First Year Puppy Health Care

Dr. Jo de Klerk

SECTION 3

Top 50 Health Problems of Puppies in the First Year of Life........ 44

Preface

I never really knew what I wanted to be when I grew up. I was into so many different things. I had a huge passion for animals, so even though studying veterinary medicine would have been the obvious choice, I came from a creative family and somehow being a vet wasn't the first thing that jumped out. Music, reading, sports, and art were all on my radar and featured heavily in my life, and so I was never the typical 'I've wanted to be a vet for as long as I can remember' type of girl.

As I journeyed through school, I explored many different careers. It wasn't so much a specific career that jumped out to me, but instead certain traits, which led me to my career choice. I loved science, and figuring out how things worked, particularly living things. I loved to teach, explain, and pass on my passions to others. I loved problem-solving and the exciting challenge of trying to figure something out. And most importantly, I loved helping others and making a difference. Those traits, combined with my dog and horse obsessions, are what led me down the path to becoming a vet.

I studied hard and was accepted into the Royal Veterinary College, which now carries the number one world ranking (I'm sure something I'll boast about until the day I die!). The five-year course was grueling and hard work, but I felt privileged to be there and pushed through in the knowledge that I would come out at the end of it in a position to make a difference to animals, people, and the world. Throughout the course, I came to realize how amazing and supportive my family and friends were, and I felt very lucky to have them.

When I approached my final year of university, I started a period of my life called 'rotations.' We were placed in groups of six students and worked as junior vets under the supervision of experienced clinicians in all the university hospitals. The first day of rotations was known as Black Monday, which described it quite well. Rotations would either make or break you. It was a fantastic learning experience though, and something I will never forget, mostly because I ended up having a film crew follow me for the whole year to add that little bit of extra stress to it!

At the start of rotations, the university was approached by a company from BBC2, which wanted to produce a documentary following students through their last year of university. The show would be called Young Vets. My friend, and fellow rotation group member, Elly, was cast for the show. On day one, the crew joined filmed her working in the Equine Hospital. She was a little nervous of horses, so she asked me to come and help. As a result, I was caught on camera quite a bit. A month later, I received a message that they had seen me in the film, and wanted to add me to the list of students who were being followed. I don't like saying no to these sorts of opportunities where they won't come around again, so I took them up on their offer without further thought. Despite the camera appearing over my shoulder constantly, making most situations highly stressful, I actually learned a lot from the whole experience. I realized it's okay not to be perfect every single time. I learned that I was actually quite good at explaining what I was doing. And I learned that I really valued the support team around me.

When the TV show was broadcast, I had some wonderful public speaking opportunities which led to being approached to write a book for publishing house Harper Collins. This was when my passion for writing ignited. I cowrote my first book with celebrity author Caro Handley, and produced a book called Tales of a Young Vet. I was so happy to be using my creative genes again, and writing all about heartwarming animal stories was great fun.

Around this time, I felt that mainstream clinical work wasn't quite for me. I enjoyed it, but I knew that I could help others more. So, I decided to plan a year of traveling and working as a vet for various different charities. I worked for World in Need in Uganda, SPANA in Morocco, and the SPCA in South Africa. Harper Collins asked me to document my travels, and on my return, we converted my diary into my second book, Tales from a Wild Vet.

The veterinary charity work was an incredible experience, and I'm so grateful to have had the opportunity to use my veterinary skills where vets were scarce. It led me to apply for my master's degree in tropical animal health. The main topic studied during this course was the subject of One Health, which is the concept that human health, animal health, and environmental health are all interconnected. This is particularly true in poor communities. My research thesis focused on how the cart horses in Cape Town impacted the lives of their owners and those that worked with them. It was eye opening and cemented my passion for using veterinary skills for those in need.

I now continue to practice clinical veterinary work in a mainstream veterinary practice as, having a young family, I am aware that putting myself in impoverished situations around the world can be dangerous. I still aim to help those in need where I can, and I frequently work with shelter dogs. I also have completed a certificate in pain management, primarily so that I can help senior, creaky animals have a better-quality life in their old age.

I love to write, and I continue to do this as a creative outlet around my clinical work. To date I have published eight books, six journal articles, hundreds of internet articles, and have written a diploma course in dog first aid. I intend to continue this for many years to come. Out of all the books I have written, First Year Puppy Health Care has been one of my favorites. Acquiring a new puppy is so exciting, and I love to share in that excitement with new owners. I hope this book will provide a wealth of information to help new puppy parents on their exciting journey with their new member of the family.

Dr. Joanna de Klerk, DVM

Research the Breeder

It's important to adopt a breed that is most suited to your lifestyle, whether that's a dog that needs a lot of exercise because you're constantly active or one who doesn't mind being alone part of the time because your work sometimes requires long hours. A bit of research right from the start will ensure you and your dog are a good match.

If you have decided on a pedigree dog, and know the breed that you are looking for, your first step is to find a breeder. If you know people who own dogs of that particular breed, ask the owners for the name of the breeder who produced their dog. Buying from a reputable, trusted breeder will help ensure you get a healthy, happy puppy.

Another ideal place to start your research is the Kennel Club website for your country. Here you will find a list of registered and approved breeders for the breed that you have in mind. In selecting a Kennel Club registered breeder, your dog will come with a comprehensive puppy pack, containing your contract of sale, your dog's registration certificate and pedigree, immunization record, worming record, and advice for continuation of care, socialization, exercise and training. You will also receive a contractual guarantee, detailing any conditions that may apply if you need to return a puppy. A Kennel Club registered breeder will commit to supporting you throughout your dog's lifetime, with advice and, if necessary, assistance in rehoming your dog should unforeseen circumstances arise.

It's worth bearing in mind that good breeders often have a waiting list for their puppies, and you may not be able to purchase right away. If you have identified a breeder whose dogs really appeal to you, however, the right dog will be worth the wait.

In some cases, the owner of a Kennel Club registered pedigree female may decide to breed a single litter from a dog with a friend's good quality Kennel Club registered

male. This informal arrangement may well result in a litter of healthy puppies that can be registered with the Kennel Club, but if you choose your dog this way, you will not necessarily have stringent health testing and guarantees or breeder support should you need it. Casual breeding also compromises the strict breed standards put in place by the Kennel Club to ensure the breeding of healthy dogs. Breeders that are not registered with the Kennel Club may still have to be licensed and inspected by the local authority if they are producing more than a certain number of litters annually, and selling their dogs for profit.

Many prospective owners prefer the idea of a cross-breed. Cross-breeds are sometimes healthier dogs, as they are less susceptible to genetic conditions from inbreeding; a benefit known as 'hybrid vigor.' Within this category are purposely bred 'designer dogs,' which are usually a cross between two distinct breeds, such as a Poodle. They still command a price tag that can be even higher than that of a pedigree dog, and often come with their own set of health issues. Also, in the crossbreed category are dogs that have a long history of totally indiscriminate breeding, resulting in a unique character, if indeterminate genetics! Neither designer breeds, cross-breeds, or Heinz-57 mongrels are recognized by the Kennel Club, so in choosing a healthy puppy you will have to rely on observation and inspection.

Wherever you find your puppy, the correct highest standards for breeding should always include prioritizing hygiene, space, and the health and welfare of parents and puppies. You should always be allowed to inspect the premises used for breeding, even if the litter is presented in a front room with the mother and siblings present. Puppy farms may look domestic and happy, while squalid kennels or sheds out the back contain the breeding stock, and fester disease. Inadvertently purchasing from a puppy farm may result in your acquiring a sickly dog, while fostering the continued suffering of an overbred bitch that will never experience family life, fresh air, good health or a break in her pregnancies.

If you have decided to rescue a dog from a shelter, it's unlikely that you will have any information on the breeder, even if it is a pedigree dog. When dogs with a registered pedigree come into a rescue, their papers are usually withheld for client confidentiality, and to prevent exploitative breeding. Just like with a breeder, it's important to do the research to ensure a rescue organization is reputable, as the health of your rescue puppy is likely to depend upon whether it has received appropriate care in the shelter, or if it has been exposed to unsanitary conditions and disease. You should look at the application process to ensure that it is sufficiently stringent to indicate that dogs are placed with the right family, and you should expect to have a home check as well as pay an adoption fee. In return, your dog should come with a vaccination record, a microchip, and a clean bill of health from a vet, having been treated for internal and external parasites. If the puppy has any health conditions, these should be made clear to you from the outset. You may also be required to neuter your puppy when he or she is old enough. The rescue should offer Rescue Back Up (RBU), which requires the new adoptive owner to return the dog to the rescue if at any point they can no longer care for it. The rescue organization's commitment to the future of your dog is a measure of how much confidence you can have in its standards for animal welfare.

Though your puppy also has 50% of his genetics from his father, you may not have the opportunity to visit him personally. This is because male stud dogs often live elsewhere. The breeder may be happy to give you the details of the father's owner for you to make an appointment to see him, but where this is not possible, you should still be able to see photographs of the father and view his pedigree. You should look carefully at the pedigrees of both parents for any names that crop up multiple times, as this indicates inbreeding, which can increase the risk of genetic health conditions. Some repetition in pedigree dogs is normal, so long as it's not excessive.

If you are intending to show your dog at any level above Companion Dog Shows at the local fair, then both parents will need to be Kennel Club registered pedigree dogs, so that your dog can also be registered with the Kennel Club in order to qualify for participation in Championship Shows.

As most genetic conditions will not reveal themselves until the puppy reaches adulthood or beyond, Kennel Club registered breeders will carry out screening to ensure that they are only breeding from healthy parents. Each breed has its own list of genetic conditions to which it may be predisposed, and the Kennel Club website lists these, so you will know which certificates to ask the breeder for. Before asking for the certificates, ensure that you read up on what a good result is on them. Some genetic tests will simply produce a 'positive' or 'negative' result for the disease, whereas others produce a score, for example elbow dysplasia, which should be as close to 0 as possible, and hip dysplasia, which should be as low as possible.

The advantage of choosing a registered breeder who screens both parents is your assurance that your puppy is not a ticking time bomb for a genetic condition. Buying a puppy without this paperwork could result in health issues later in life, even if the parents seem fine, because some dogs may be carriers of a condition without showing symptoms themselves. When two parent carriers breed, there is a 25% chance of the puppy being clear, a 50% chance of being a carrier, and a 25% chance of developing the condition.

You should ask to see the certificates for the health screening procedures both parents have had. Even if the father is not present, the breeder should still be able to produce his certificates.

Viewing the Puppies

Sometimes you will not be able to view the parents; for example, if a litter has been dumped and taken into rescue. In this case you will have to rely on physical inspection of the puppy to ensure that he is healthy. And even when you have seen the parents, along with their pedigrees, screening certificates and veterinary records, there are still important factors to look out for in selecting a healthy puppy from the litter.

The first consideration is whether you wish to have a male or female. In general, males are more boisterous than females and slightly larger when fully grown. There will be different health issues relating to each gender; for example, males may be susceptible to prostate problems, and females to a womb infection known

as pyometra, mammary tumors and hormonal issues associated with their seasons. Whether you choose a male or female, neutering or spaying your dog will prevent these issues if you do not intend to breed from him or her.

All the puppies in the litter should appear lively and be interacting with each other. Many people say that rather than picking the first puppy that comes to you, or the sad one in the corner, you should look for the dog in the middle of these two extremes. A very confident dog may turn out to be dominant, and a quiet dog may have anxiety or health issues. So, if you want to play it safe, you should look for the middle ground. The breeder should allow you to handle all the dogs, not only to see which puppy you connect with, but to check that they are physically healthy.

When you pick up a puppy, you should check that he is clean, especially around his bottom, and that he doesn't smell. His coat should feel plush and silky with no scabs or encrustations, and his eyes should be bright and clear and free of any discharge. His ears should also be clean and not smell. His nose should be cold, clean and slightly wet, and his gums should be pink. His tummy should be plump but not hard or distended, which may indicate a worm problem, and he should not have any fleas. The puppy should not have any visible ribs and should not be limping or have labored breathing. You should check his tummy for a lump indicating an umbilical hernia, and if he is a boy, you should feel for two testes in the scrotum. Be aware that up until eight weeks of age, both testicles may not yet have dropped, so this may be something to check back on when you collect your puppy.

Although you may visit your puppy for the first time from around five weeks of age, the breeder should not allow you to take him home before he is eight weeks and fully weaned. Under UK law, a puppy must be microchipped by eight weeks. Other countries such as the USA may not legally require microchipping, but it's a good idea to help ensure a swift reunion if he ever goes missing.

Having taken so much care in selecting a healthy puppy, you will be off to the best possible start. That said, pet insurance is definitely something to consider. This will ensure that your dog will always receive the medical care he needs, and there will not be any nasty financial surprises around the corner.

SECTION ②

Your Puppy's Health Requirements Over the First Year

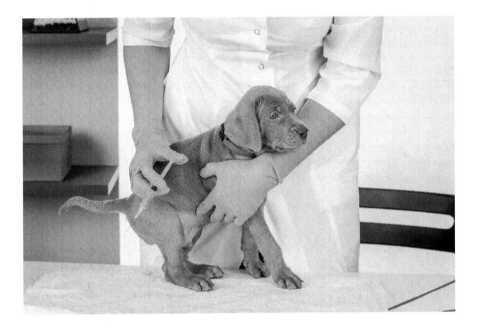

8 WEEKS TO 3 MONTHS

Vaccinations

The first time you take your new puppy to the vet will probably be for his first vaccination. This is a great opportunity not only to provide your puppy with the best preventative healthcare but also to discuss any concerns with your vet, as well as introduce your puppy to the idea of being examined. Most veterinary practices use vaccination consults as an opportunity to carry out a clinical examination of your puppy, discuss parasite control and nutrition, and address any concerns. You might also find yourself talking about microchipping, plans for neutering, and even advice on what pet insurance to take out.

There are several vaccinations which your puppy needs to have in this timeframe, and you may find that the breeder has already taken him to have his first injection if you've only picked the dog up at 10, 11 or 12 weeks old. Each veterinary practice has a different schedule for the first set of vaccines, but most consist of two or three vaccinations, each spaced three to four weeks apart, such as at 8, 12 and 16 weeks of age.

The youngest age that a puppy should receive a vaccination is eight weeks old. This is because when a puppy suckles milk from its mother, maternally derived antibodies (MDAs) transfer from the milk into the puppy. This enables puppies to have some form of immunity, while they are still building their own. However, the MDAs stay in the dog's system and interfere with vaccinations until eight weeks of age, and sometimes even later. This means if a vaccination is given before this time, it might be ineffective.

Vaccinations are inactive forms of the pathogen which causes whatever disease is being vaccinated against. They do not cause the disease in your puppy, but your puppy's immune system recognizes that it should not be there and attacks it. After this, 'memory cells' remain behind, ready to replicate instantly if challenged again with the same thing. As a result, if your puppy comes into contact with the pathogen again after being fully vaccinated, he's unlikely to get sick.

There are two different types of vaccinations; core vaccines and non-core vaccines. All dogs, regardless of lifestyle and geographical area, should receive core vaccinations. Non-core vaccines, on the other hand, are dependent on whether certain diseases are present in your area of the country, and the lifestyle of your dog; for example, if he socializes with other dogs while out walking, or stays in kennels when you are on vacation. Core vaccines are usually combined into one injection, and non-core vaccines are typically additional injections.

Core Vaccines

- **Distemper**: This is a virus which causes non-specific symptoms, such as sneezing, vomiting, and coughing. It can also cause hardening and thickening of the pads on the paws and of the nose. It rapidly progresses to death.

- **Parvovirus:** This virus primarily affects dogs under a year old, especially young puppies. It causes bloody diarrhea, which is extremely contagious. This gradually causes puppies to fade due to dehydration and blood loss.

- **Canine Adenovirus:** This virus causes hepatitis. It can cause vague symptoms such as fatigue, fever, vomiting, diarrhea and jaundice, and it will rapidly lead to death.

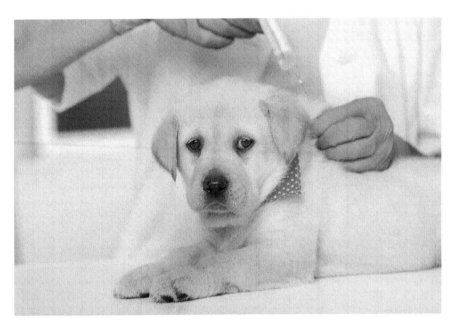

Non-Core Vaccines

- **Leptospirosis:** This disease is a type of bacteria with several serotypes (variations). Different vaccines cover different serotypes, and so you should inquire which vaccine your vet uses. Leptospirosis causes failure of the kidneys and liver, and the most common symptom is yellowing of the gums and eyes, known as jaundice. Some dogs also display neurological symptoms, such as loss of balance and seizures.

- **Parainfluenza:** This is sometimes mixed with the core vaccine injection, or it can be part of the kennel cough vaccine, explained below. Parainfluenza is a virus, which can lead to a debilitating cough.

- **Kennel cough:** This vaccine contains Bordetella and Parainfluenza. Together, these two viruses create a complex disease known as kennel cough. It is highly contagious and causes a honking cough and a fever. This vaccine is squirted up the nose rather than injected.

- **Rabies:** This injection should be given as standard to any dog which lives in a rabies endemic area, as well as to any dog traveling to a rabies endemic area. It is a dangerous disease which causes aggression, hypersalivation and neurological symptoms, which lead to death. If a rabid dog bites a human, he or she also may contract the fatal disease.

Worming

Worms are parasites that live inside your puppy's gastrointestinal system. They can be picked up from other puppies, your puppy's mother, or simply your puppy's environment where there could be fecal or saliva contamination.

Two different types of worms must be routinely treated in young puppies: roundworms and tapeworms. Roundworms can be anywhere from microscopic up to a couple of inches long, whereas tapeworms can potentially grow to yards in length. Both feed off the nutrients your puppy eats, essentially stealing them from him. As a result, worms can make your puppy thin even though he is receiving enough calories. They can also cause the intestines to become inflamed, which worsens the issue, as inflamed intestines do not allow for nutrients to be properly absorbed into the bloodstream.

The breeder should deworm your puppy with a broad-spectrum roundworm treatment every two weeks. Once the puppy reaches eight weeks old, he can have his first combined roundworm and tapeworm treatment. This is usually in the form of a tablet. From then on, he should be treated every three to six months for tapeworms, and monthly until at least six months old, for roundworms.

Treatment can come in a variety of forms. Praziquantel, a treatment for tapeworms, is almost always prescribed as tablets or medicated chews; however, roundworm treatments can also come in the form of a pipette. These are easy to use by just parting the hair on the back of your dog's neck and squeezing the contents onto the skin.

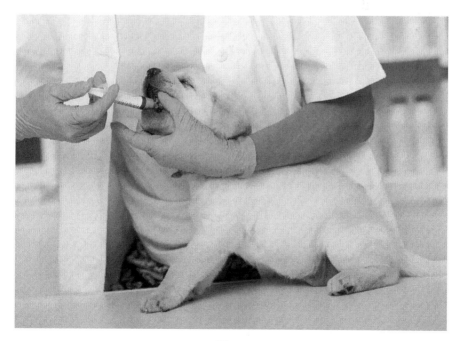

Ecto-Parasite Control

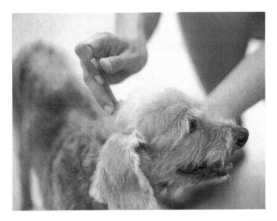

Ecto-parasites are any parasites which live on the outside of your puppy. These include fleas, ticks, mites, ear mites, and lice. Most of them will only cause your puppy to itch, but some can carry more sinister diseases, so it is important not only to treat them but to also prevent them. In some areas of the world, ticks can carry deadly diseases such as Babesia, Ehrlichia, and Anaplasma, and fleas can carry tapeworms.

Ecto-parasite control can come in a variety of different forms and different lengths of residual action, varying from no ongoing protection, to up to six months of protection. Forms include tablets, injections, medicated treats, shampoos, collars, sprays, and spot-on pipettes. You should always buy these products from your veterinarian, as medications from the supermarket or pet shop are not always effective, due to a build-up of resistance in the parasite population. The application frequency will depend on what sort of product you have chosen to use, but it can sometimes be difficult to remember when to apply these products if you're not used to having to remember things for a puppy. It can be very useful to invest in a wall calendar and mark when you need to next apply the treatment. Some ecto-parasite treatments even come with stickers for you to put in your calendar!

Young Puppy Exercise

There are a lot of schools of thought about the influence of exercise on a puppy's health. It's generally agreed between veterinarians and breeders that puppies shouldn't be exercised too much, but there's no official formula to say how much is overdoing it.

It's believed that over-exercising puppies can lead to joint and bone developmental abnormalities, especially if your puppy is a large breed dog. Each puppy is an individual though, and some breeds may require more mental stimulation than others, and therefore, making sensible judgments based on knowledge of your puppy's breed is the best way forward. A general rule of thumb is to not let your puppy exercise for more than five minutes of exercise per month of age. This can be done up to twice daily.

At this stage, between eight weeks and three months, your puppy will not have yet finished his course of vaccinations, so exercising him in public is not recommended. He will be at a higher risk of contracting these avoidable diseases, so he should only be exercised on your private property or the property of friends who have fully vaccinated dogs.

When exercising your puppy, variation will help keep him entertained as well as reduce the chances of health risks associated with repetitive exercise. Exercise doesn't always have to mean going for a walk; it can include playing, swimming, leash training, puppy classes and exploring.

Pet Insurance

Protecting yourself from unexpected vet bills from the get-go is a wise idea. If your puppy becomes ill, gets injured or has an emergency, veterinary costs can come as an unexpected shock. Sometimes these costs are astronomical and bills can run into thousands of dollars. By having pet insurance, you can be assured that if something terrible happens, your puppy's health care will be covered.

Taking out pet insurance while your puppy is still young ensures the best coverage. Puppies usually have relatively little medically wrong with them, so the risks for the insurance company are small. As a result, your premium will be cheaper. If you wait until your puppy is older, and has already made some visits to the vet, the insurance company might evaluate your dog's medical history and place exclusions on your policy based on any past issues.

There are numerous pet insurance providers on the market, all claiming to give your dog the best or most affordable health cover. But there are subtle differences and clauses between different providers, so it is worth doing your research. For many insurance companies there are three levels of coverage:

- Accident coverage
- Accident and illness coverage
- Accident, illness and routine care coverage (which includes contributions towards vaccinations, parasite control, neutering, and dental care)

In addition to this, there may be differences in the specific way insurance companies offer coverage. Some might offer a sum of money per condition per year, and others might offer a sum of money per condition for the lifetime of your dog, whereas others might offer a sum of money for all conditions for a year. Therefore, reading the fine print is important to understand what you are signing up for. It's also important to note that many insurance companies do not cover congenital diseases or birth defects.

Some people feel that paying into an insurance fund is like throwing money away, so they open a pet savings account instead. They put a dedicated amount aside each month into this savings account, or top it up whenever they have a bonus or a good month. However, the reality is, while saving for a rainy day is a good idea, this sum of money is unlikely to come close to what you might need if your dog develops a chronic condition or suffers an acute illness or accident. For many owners, pet insurance will pay for itself and more, and those fortunate enough to rarely need to make a claim at least have peace of mind.

Microchipping

Microchipping is recommended for all dogs, and in the UK, it has now become a legal requirement. Though it is not yet a legal requirement in the USA, it is highly recommended. A microchip is a small piece of metal, about the size of a grain of rice, that is inserted under a dog's skin in between the shoulder blades. When the chip is scanned by a reader, it gives a number, which can then be looked up with the microchip company. The number is unique and your contact information will be registered to the number so it is important to remember to update the chip if you move house or change cell phone numbers.

This chip is inserted with a needle, like an injection, which might make your dog yelp briefly. However, the pain is very short-lived. If you are concerned about your puppy being injected with a microchip at a young age (unless you're in the UK, where all dogs must be microchipped by eight weeks old), you can opt to have him injected while under anesthesia when he's neutered.

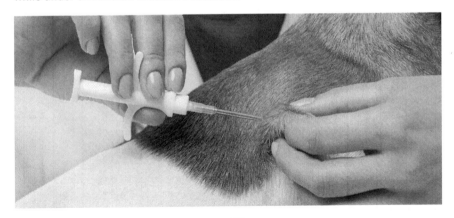

Nutrition

Striding into a pet store, anticipating the new arrival of your puppy can both be exciting and overwhelming. One of the decisions you might start to think about while shopping is what sort of food you would like to buy for your puppy. You may notice that a large proportion of the pet store's shelves are stocked with dog food, from kibble to canned food, to treats. Pet store assistants are often fairly knowledgeable and are a good source of information, as is your veterinarian. So, if the decision of what to feed your new puppy is difficult, be sure to seek out some professional advice.

As a general rule, when a puppy is first brought home, feeding him the same diet which the breeder was giving him will prevent any early stomach upsets. Sudden changes can irritate a puppy's sensitive stomach and may cause transient vomiting or diarrhea, so it is best to feed the same diet as the breeder for several days, then gradually change over to his new diet, mixing it with his old diet, over the course of one to two weeks.

When choosing what diet to move your puppy over to, there are several factors you can consider:

Life Stage

At this age, your puppy should be fed a 'puppy' or 'junior' diet. These diets are high in protein, calcium and phosphorus, ideal for growing muscles and bones. Feeding an adult food, instead of a food for younger dogs, may stunt a puppy's growth or cause brittle bones.

Breed or Size Specific

Some brands of food offer diets tailored to specific breeds or sizes of dogs, such as large-breed dogs. It is not essential to feed a highly specific food for Miniature Poodle puppies, for example, but the benefit of these foods is that a great deal of research has gone into exactly what quantities of nutrients are ideal for this breed, as well as the appropriate kibble size.

Type of Food

There are three types of food; dry food (kibble), wet food (canned) and home-prepared food. Puppies should never be fed home-prepared diets as it is extremely difficult to provide the appropriate quantities of calcium and phosphorus for bones to grow adequately. This is explained further in 'Nutritional Deficiencies' in Section 3.

Dry foods are more condensed than wet foods, and therefore you will not have to feed as many grams of dry food as you would wet food to ensure your puppy gets all the nutrients he needs. Because dry food is more condensed than wet food, it can swell when it hits the stomach acid, leaving your puppy feeling bloated or needing to go potty in the night.

Dry kibble can come in a variety of sizes. The general rule is that you should buy the biggest kibble that your dog will eat, which at this stage is probably still quite small. If the kibble pieces are large, your dog must crunch through them before swallowing, helping the teeth to have a regular source of abrasion, which reduces the amount of tartar build-up and promotes healthier teeth.

Wet food, on the other hand, does not provide abrasion on the teeth, and therefore your puppy is much more likely to develop dental disease. Nevertheless, there is a place for wet food in a dog's diet. Wet food is usually more palatable than dry food, so if your puppy is a picky eater, then he is likely to eat more wet food than dry food.

Ingredients

All dog foods must list the ingredients in descending order of percentage. Therefore, the first ingredient has the most in the recipe. Ideally, the first ingredient should be a meat protein source, which is a pure meat and not offal or by-products, and should make up a large proportion of the recipe. Common meat ingredients include beef, chicken, lamb, and fish, and your puppy may prefer the taste of specific ones or not be fussy. You might also prefer the smell of certain dog foods over others!

Other ingredients in dog food include grains, vegetables, and added minerals, vitamins and probiotics. Grains are an excellent source of fiber, which helps keep your puppy's digestion working well, and vegetables are wonderful natural sources of a variety of vitamins. Nothing should sound chemical in the list of ingredients! The more natural ingredients, the better.

Dental Care

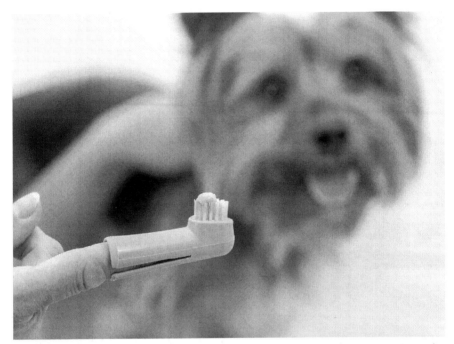

Keeping your puppy's teeth clean is important from the very beginning. Once the health of the mouth has become compromised, saving teeth from loss and decay is extremely difficult. Prevention is always better than cure. Teaching your dog to tolerate dental care from a young age will make your life much easier when it comes to looking after his teeth. With patience and practice, you can even make dental hygiene a fun experience for your puppy.

Teeth Brushing

Teeth brushing should be the main preventative measure that all owners should take. This will help keep teeth clean and stop tartar build-up. The teeth should always be brushed with dog toothpaste, as human toothpaste can be toxic to dogs. Dogs also much prefer the meaty flavor of dog toothpaste. Toothpaste formulated for dogs has enzymes in it which help to dissolve any tartar which has started to build up.

There are several options for brushing tools. While you can buy dog toothbrushes, your puppy will probably prefer you to use a rubber finger brush in his small mouth. Brushing should be done daily to get the best effect. Start with the incisors at the front, then the canines, then pull the cheeks back to reach the back molars and premolars. Don't expect brushing to be accepted by your puppy immediately. He is likely to wriggle, but ensure that you make it a fun experience, with plenty of positive reinforcement.

Dental Chews

Dental chews are an easy way of keeping your dog's teeth healthy, but they are not a replacement for brushing. The idea behind the chews is that they suck off the tartar as the tooth sinks into it. Dental chews contain calories, and therefore it is important to remember that any calories which are given in the form of treats are calculated into your puppy's daily caloric intake so you can adapt his meal portions accordingly.

Some owners prefer natural chews for their dogs, including bones and antlers. While this helps to create abrasion on the teeth and scrape off tartar, such chews should not be given to puppies, who have fragile teeth and could easily fracture them.

Dental Wash

Dog dental mouthwash is becoming increasingly popular. As with the toothpaste, the enzymes help to dissolve the tartar off the teeth. It's easy to use—simply add it to your dog's water every day. Never give your dog human mouthwash, as, like human toothpaste, it can be toxic and lead to liver damage.

The water with added mouthwash should be completely replaced with fresh water daily. This will ensure the enzymes in the mouthwash are working efficiently, as well as provide your dog with fresh water. Mouthwash is less effective than brushing, so do not substitute one for the other.

The Importance of 'Stay'

'Sit' and 'Stay' are the first commands you will learn in puppy training classes, and if you have not trained a dog before, it is worth attending classes to cement these important commands in your dog's brain, as well as to have moral support while you turn your dog into a model citizen.

Modern dog training is taught using positive reinforcement, which rewards a dog for a correct action. Punishment is never used, as it makes a dog fearful and undermines your relationship. So, in the early months of training your dog, you will be used to having a pocket or fanny pack full of small training treats. Some training classes also use a clicker to reinforce positive behavior in the dog's mind. If you do not attend classes, you can find useful training videos online to help you teach the basic commands. It is important to be consistent in your methods, whichever you may choose.

'Stay' is especially important near busy roads. It may also be used in the presence of other potential dangers, such as unknown dogs or cattle, or to protect others from the unwanted attentions of your dog, such as small children. It is a truly disciplined dog, however, that can be commanded to 'Stay' when a cat, squirrel or rabbit crosses its path. Some breeds have a very strong, primal prey drive, so you will have to judge your own dog's level of obedience in deciding when a leash may be necessary, especially near cliffs and roads.

The Importance of 'Leave It'

'Leave it' is another useful command when you may need to override your dog's instincts to chase, or when you find something you wish him to leave alone on a walk, or if your dog needs to accept and respect small household pets. Most critically, however, when it comes to the health of your dog, the 'Leave It' command is vital to stop him from gobbling down some scavenged decaying morsel that you know will upset his tummy!

You can use training treats to teach 'Leave It.' With your dog in the 'Sit' or the 'Lie Down' position, get his full attention on you, then put a treat between, or in front of, his front legs. Cover it with your hand if necessary, and command him to 'Leave It' by encouraging eye contact between you. Don't prolong the wait beyond what you believe your dog can bear, as you need to end the exercise by permitting him to 'Take It.' With steady repetition, you can extend the period between 'Leave It' and 'Take It.' Then, with your dog in the 'Lie Down' position, place a treat on each paw, and command him to 'Leave It' until you give him permission. This party trick always impresses visitors, but it also fulfills an important health and safety purpose in keeping your dog from harm in certain situations.

Older Puppy Exercise

Once your puppy has completed his first vaccinations, you can begin to exercise him out in public. The guideline of five minutes of exercise per month of age twice daily still applies, but now you can take him to more exciting places to explore. The length of the walk should be increased gradually, to prevent sudden changes. It will also help to take frequent breaks as you walk so that your puppy is not constantly running. Remember, repetitive exercise can put his developing joints at increased risk. If you are particularly worried about damaging his joints, or your puppy is a breed which is particularly at risk of joint dysplasia (further discussed in Section 3), then there are several things you can do to minimize the chances of something happening.

First, and most importantly, teach your puppy to walk on a leash. This is a useful tool for you to use when your puppy starts to get carried away. If he is charging around with no control, then a short period of time on the leash will allow him to calm down and focus on you. You need to have realistic expectations when first training your puppy to walk on the leash. In order to maintain his focus, you will not be going consistently in one direction or at one speed. You will also have to work to keep your puppy's full attention by being more exciting than his surroundings. To your puppy, the leash prevents him from going where he wants, so he will instinctively pull. He needs to disassociate pulling with getting where he wants, and associate going forward with the feel of a loose leash. So, every time he pulls, you need to stop. Put your puppy in the sit so that you can regain a loose leash, then proceed. Your walk is going to be a continual sequence of stopping and starting in the early stages, and you should also keep changing direction to keep your dog interested. Eventually, he will realize there is a lot more walking and a lot less stopping and sitting when the leash is loose, and he will learn that the right place to be is by your side. Keep your training treats handy so you can reward correct behavior when he is walking nicely.

Another top tip to protect your puppy's joints is to avoid walking on the hottest and coldest parts of the day, and only take him for walks in areas that aren't slippery. Sudden jerks from a slip or fall can lead to injury, which in turn can affect your puppy's development. If you're worried at all and your puppy appears to be limping, the best thing to do is to take him to the vet.

Parasite Control

Continual parasite control, throughout the three-to-six-month age range, for worms and ecto-parasites is very important to ensure your puppy stays in good health. Deworming for roundworms should continue monthly until six months of age. When your puppy reaches six months, you can give him another roundworm and tapeworm combination treatment.

As before, ecto-parasite treatment should be continual, to ensure that you are not only treating infestations but also preventing them.

Nail Clipping

Now that your puppy is a few months old, his little nails are probably becoming longer. If you are walking him on a variety of surfaces, you might find that they wear down naturally, but excessive walking on hard surfaces is not recommended for a puppy's growing joints. Therefore, you might find that your puppy's nails require a trim.

Some dogs find that nail clipping is scary. Some don't like the noise, whereas others have had a previous bad experience. Therefore, start by getting your puppy used to the idea slowly. Playing with his paws daily, holding them and picking them up, will make him more tolerant of you fiddling around when it comes to nail clipping.

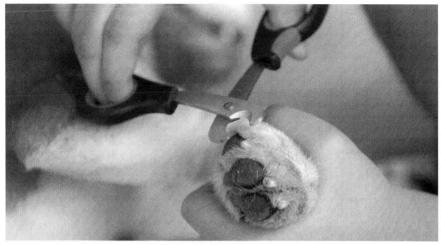

Buy a nail clipper from your local pet store. These come in a variety of sizes, but a smaller one will be most appropriate for your puppy at this stage, as he will only have small, soft nails. As your puppy grows, you may need to invest in a bigger nail clipper, because the nails will become thicker and harder.

The nails are made out of keratin, much like our nails. In the center is a fleshy quick, which contains nerves and blood vessels. If the nails are cut too short, then it is easy to catch the quick and cause the nail to bleed. This can be very painful, and a bad experience like this is something your puppy may remember for next time. If your dog has clear nails, you can usually see the quick, but if they are black it can be much harder to determine where it is. For some dogs, you can turn the paw upside down, as sometimes the keratin does not completely enclose the quick, and therefore you can see it. For other dogs though, the keratin can completely enclose it, and all you can do is slowly and carefully cut small bits off. You can use a nail file or nail grinder if you find this easier, although not all puppies have the tolerance to wait while their nails are filed. If you do accidentally catch the quick, do not panic, and just apply firm pressure with a wad of cotton wool for five minutes.

If you don't feel confident enough to trim your dog's nails yourself, your local veterinarian or groomer will be happy to assist.

First Trip to the Groomer

Taking your puppy to the groomer for the first time can be like taking your child for his first haircut. It is a momentous occasion, and this first trip will set him up for how he feels about the groomer for the rest of his life. Therefore, it is imperative that it is a positive experience.

Part of ensuring that your puppy has a positive experience is to choose a reputable groomer. Do your research before booking the appointment, and set up a visit to scope out the facilities beforehand. Things to look out for include cleanliness and a clean smell, a well-lit environment, friendly and knowledgeable staff who listen to your concerns and answer your questions, and evidence that pets are monitored continuously when waiting in the kennels.

Before the visit, you can acclimate your puppy to some of the processes which will happen at the groomer. This includes playing with his paws, handling his ears, rinsing him off with water, brushing his coat, and familiarizing him with the sounds of clippers (you can use beard clippers) and blow dryers.

A good groomer will help make the experience a positive one for your puppy. They should talk to your puppy in a gentle and calm voice, and if you are allowed to stay to help, then you should try to do this too. Acting anxious or excited yourself will only agitate your puppy. Giving your puppy a small training treat occasionally will ensure that he creates a positive association with the process, or if you are not allowed to stay, or you think you will make your puppy anxious, then leave the treats with the groomer. If you leave your puppy at the groomer, ensure that you don't make your goodbye emotional. This will make your dog worry that something bad might happen.

Often the first session might just be a bath and a brush, getting the puppy used to being at the groomer's. Then the next session might include some areas of hair trimming. It's likely a full trim will only happen after several visits, and ear cleaning, ear plucking, and anal gland expression might only be added in several months later.

When you are done, make sure to book routine appointments on the advice of the groomer for your specific puppy. This will ensure his coat, nails, ears, and anal glands are kept in good health.

6 TO 12 MONTHS

Neutering

If you are not planning on breeding your dog, it is for his benefit to get him neutered. Many breeders require neutering in their contracts. For female dogs, this is called spaying, and for male dogs, it is called castration. There are pros and cons of both, but for most dogs, the pros outweigh the cons.

The procedures for both males and females require a day visit to the vet. You will need to bring in your dog early in the morning, having not had breakfast, and the operation will usually be done by lunchtime. The dog will then spend the afternoon recovering and sleeping off the remainder of the anesthetic before being allowed to go home. Neutering can be done any time after six months of age; however, for females, there can be some benefits to delaying spaying for a few months.

Spaying

A female dog can be spayed at any time; however, most vets agree that it should either be done before the first estrus at six months old, or three months after the first estrus, which can be as old as 18 months. Reducing the risk of developing mammary tumors is one reasons many vets advocate for spaying. Mammary tumors are hormonally driven, and canine mammary tumor cells carry both estrogen and progesterone receptors. Spaying to prevent mammary tumors is time-dependent and must be carried out before 2.5 years of age. If spaying is performed before the first estrus, there is a 0.5% chance of a mammary tumor developing, before the second estrus, an 8% chance, and after the second estrus, a 26% chance.

Another reason for spaying is that it eliminates the possibility of a condition called pyometra. This is a potentially life-threatening infection of the uterus. Approximately 24% of female dogs that are not spayed will develop pyometra at some point in

You can also begin to get him used to some agility equipment. Dogs under a year should never attempt objects such as the teeter or A-frame, but getting him used to moving objects, such as a large piece of plywood with a small plank of wood underneath to make it see-saw, is a great alternative. Your pup can also be introduced to weaving through widely spaced weave poles and traveling through tunnels.

The most important thing at this stage is that you build your puppy's confidence, so these sessions should always be positive and contain plenty of rewards. They should also always be kept short to avoid any over-excitement or damage to your puppy's joints.

Parasite Control

Parasite control for worms and ecto-parasites from six months old is very similar to the treatment your puppy received earlier in his life. Ensuring there are no gaps between treatments is vital to your dog's continuing health.

In some areas of the world, you can reduce your monthly roundworm treatments to once every three months. If you live in areas where heartworm or lungworm is endemic, however, you must still provide monthly treatment. If you are not sure, it is best to talk to your vet for advice.

Weight Management

As your dog grows and starts to reach full size, his diet will change. This is a good time to start researching junior adult dog foods to transition your dog over to once he is a year old. If he remains on puppy food after this, he may receive too many calories and begin to gain weight in the form of fat, instead of muscle and bone.

Neutering also contributes to weight gain as it changes the metabolism of your dog. Castrating males triples the risk of obesity, and spaying females increases the risk from 1.6 to 2 times. Obesity can have many health implications, including increased stress on the joints, heart, and liver, so once your dog is neutered, you should slightly decrease the amount of food you are feeding him, and monitor his weight carefully. In Section 3, this is discussed further, as well as how to 'Body Condition Score' your dog.

SUMMARY

Whether you have a puppy for the first time or have had numerous puppies in your lifetime, the healthcare requirements in your puppy's first year can seem extensive. However, getting this right will set him up for a healthy adult life, full of vitality.

The experts surrounding you and your puppy, such as your puppy's veterinarian, veterinary nurse, breeder, and groomer, are all excellent resources for information that will help you give your puppy the best start possible, so don't be afraid to ask questions and advice. By doing this, and combining it with the information in this book, your puppy is sure to be as healthy as can be.

SECTION ③

Top 50 Health Problems of Puppies in the First Year of Life

Angular Limb Deformities

About the Condition

Abnormal development of the forelimb bones, such as the radius and ulnar, can cause the forelimbs to grow at incorrect angles. This can happen for two reasons; it can be congenital, or it can happen because of an injury to the growth plate at the end of each long bone, when your puppy is very young. You are likely to only first notice it as your puppy grows and starts reaching the middle of his first year of life.

The abnormal development of the bones can cause short legs, bowing legs or twisting at the level of the carpus (wrist), which causes the paws to point outwards.

Quick Facts

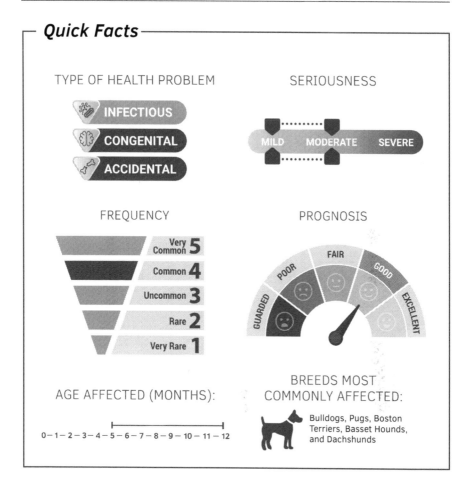

TYPE OF HEALTH PROBLEM

INFECTIOUS

CONGENITAL

ACCIDENTAL

SERIOUSNESS

MILD   MODERATE   SEVERE

FREQUENCY

Very Common **5**

Common **4**

Uncommon **3**

Rare **2**

Very Rare **1**

PROGNOSIS

GUARDED   POOR   FAIR   GOOD   EXCELLENT

AGE AFFECTED (MONTHS):

0 − 1 − 2 − 3 − 4 − 5 − 6 − 7 − 8 − 9 − 10 − 11 − 12

BREEDS MOST COMMONLY AFFECTED:

Bulldogs, Pugs, Boston Terriers, Basset Hounds, and Dachshunds

Clinical Signs

Mild

• Intermittent uneven steps

Moderate

• Pain
• Lameness
• Reduced flexion and extension of the joints

Diagnosis

Your veterinarian will perform an orthopedic exam to understand the extent of the problem. He will check how easily your dog's legs move and whether they are painful.

An X-ray will be able to determine the extent of the deformity, and help plan for surgical correction.

Treatment

Home Management

All dogs with orthopedic problems, no matter how young, should be given joint supplements containing glucosamine and omega oils. These help to protect the cartilage and joint fluid, enabling the joints to stay fully functional and well lubricated when they have abnormal weight bearing due to the malformed legs.

Medical Management

If your dog's limb deformity is uncomfortable, your veterinarian may prescribe anti-inflammatories to decrease the pain.

Surgical Management

Surgical correction is the ideal treatment, and the aim is to correct the shape and length of the limb, to enable the joints to move normally. Each surgery is different depending on the dog, but usually internal or external implants are required to keep the correction in place.

Prognosis

For mild and moderate angular limb deformities, the prognosis for the future is good with surgical correction. If it is not corrected, the extra stress which is placed on the joints from a deformed leg will lead to early-onset arthritis and pain.

Aortic Stenosis

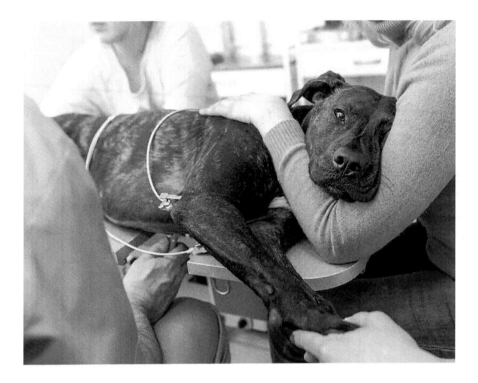

About the Condition

Aortic stenosis occurs when the left-hand side of the heart is impeded from empty-ing adequately due to a narrowing of the area around the aortic valve. The valve is positioned at the exit of the heart to prevent backflow of blood when it is pumped out towards the body. The narrowing can be above or below the valve, as well as the valve itself.

As a result of the condition, the left side of the heart must contract harder to pump out the required amount of blood, which leads to an overdevelopment of the heart muscle. This can be dangerous, as when the heart muscle grows, the blood supply in the small vessels leading to it may be insufficient. Therefore, if the stenosis is not addressed, the muscle cells can die from lack of oxygen and energy. In extreme cas-es, this can lead to abnormal heartbeat (arrhythmia) and heart attacks.

Quick Facts

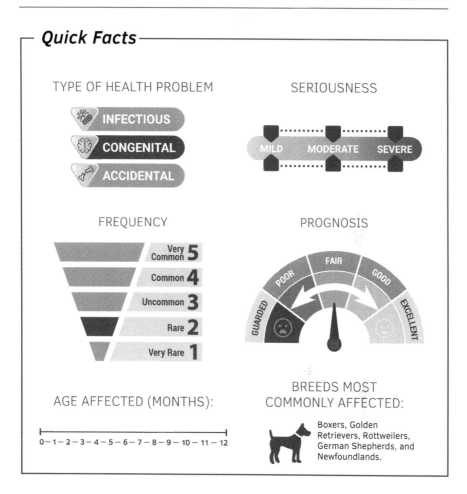

TYPE OF HEALTH PROBLEM

INFECTIOUS

CONGENITAL

ACCIDENTAL

SERIOUSNESS

MILD   MODERATE   SEVERE

FREQUENCY

Very Common **5**
Common **4**
Uncommon **3**
Rare **2**
Very Rare **1**

PROGNOSIS

POOR   FAIR   GOOD

GUARDED   EXCELLENT

AGE AFFECTED (MONTHS):

0 – 1 – 2 – 3 – 4 – 5 – 6 – 7 – 8 – 9 – 10 – 11 – 12

BREEDS MOST COMMONLY AFFECTED:

Boxers, Golden Retrievers, Rottweilers, German Shepherds, and Newfoundlands.

Clinical Signs

Mild

- Lethargy
- Heart murmur (to be detected by a vet)

Moderate

- Exercise intolerance
- Fainting

Severe

- Weak femoral pulses (severe cases)
- Arrhythmia

Diagnosis

Aortic stenosis can be diagnosed with an ultrasound scan (echocardiography) of the heart. This will also rule out other heart conditions with similar symptoms. Your vet may take X-rays of the heart, which will show an enlarged left side and dilation of the aorta; the blood vessel into which the left side of the heart pumps. If there is an arrhythmia, an electrocardiogram (ECG) will investigate the severity, and determine the risk of sudden death.

Treatment

There are three options for treatment: medical management, balloon valvuloplasty and open-heart surgery.

Medical Management

Medical management involves giving medications that reduce the demand of the heart muscle for oxygen, prolong the relaxed stage of the heartbeat to ensure it fills with blood fully, and reduce stress on the muscular wall of the heart. These medications may also be combined with anti-arrhythmia drugs if required.

Surgical Management

Balloon valvuloplasty is when a catheter is inserted into the heart from a vein, and once in place, is inflated to expand the aortic valve area. This is very effective in the short term, and carries fewer risks than open-heart surgery, but the effects may be inconsistent in the long term.

Open-heart surgery to expand the aortic valve area, or bypass it, is costly and can only be performed by experienced veterinary cardiologists. The surgery is high risk, but has a good long-term outcome.

Prognosis

In dogs which only have a mild form of the condition, the prognosis is fair to good. Some can even be managed with no treatment at all, and just careful monitoring. Severe cases, however, carry a much poorer prognosis if left without intervention. Affected dogs should never be bred.

Diagnosis

Diagnosis of a bee sting is often by examination and how your puppy is acting. He may be whimpering, rubbing his face on furniture, or licking the affected part of his body. In most cases, that is all that will be noticeable. For some dogs, however, like humans, a bee sting may cause an anaphylactic reaction. Again, this is obvious by the outward symptoms, and no further diagnostics are necessary.

Treatment

Treatment for bee stings will vary depending on the severity of the symptoms.

Home Management

If your puppy is just mildly uncomfortable, putting an ice pack on the area will help bring down the swelling and discomfort. You should look for a stinger, and remove it if you see one. This should be done by scraping it out with something flat, such as a credit card, as if it is squeezed, for example if you try to pinch it out with tweezers, it can release more venom into the skin.

Medical Management

If you see swelling of the head or neck, difficulty breathing or coughing, difficulty swallowing or seizures, you must take your puppy immediately to the nearest veterinarian, as these are all signs of an anaphylactic reaction. The main concern about reactions of this nature is that the airway becomes blocked, and your puppy suffocates. Medications will be immediately administered to open up the airways and decrease the reaction, and may be combined with intubating the airways to keep them open.

Surgical Management

In very rare cases, the airway may be too closed up to pass a tube. In this case, a tracheostomy may need to be placed. This is when an incision is made into the windpipe from the neck, into which a tube is placed directly for your puppy to breathe through. This allows time for the swelling of the larynx (top of the throat) to go down.

Prognosis

For mild cases, the prognosis is excellent, and with home care your puppy should be comfortable again in 24-48 hours. For severe anaphylactic reactions, the prognosis is good, as long as you reach the emergency vet swiftly.

Blocked Tear Ducts

About the Condition

Tears are produced to lubricate the eye. Without them, the eyes would be sticky, itchy and dry. Two tear ducts drain the tears from the eye to stop them from overflowing. They sit in the middle corner of the eye, and are based in the top and bottom eyelid. The openings to the tear ducts are called the inferior and superior lacrimal puncta.

A congenital condition, called imperforate lacrimal puncta, can be present from birth. This occurs when the openings to the tear ducts are blocked off by a thin layer of skin. It is sometimes not apparent in a newborn puppy, and you may only notice it when you bring your puppy home for the first time and see the tears overflow onto the face because the tear ducts are closed.

Quick Facts

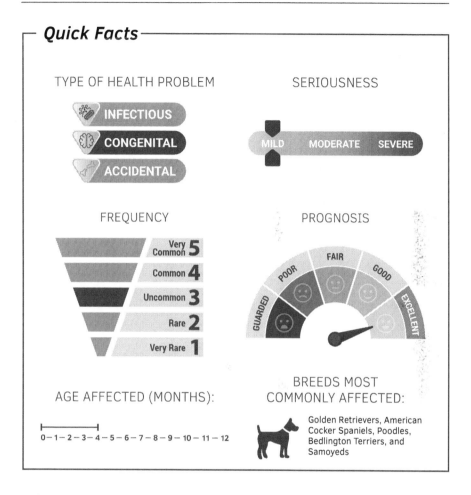

TYPE OF HEALTH PROBLEM

- INFECTIOUS
- CONGENITAL
- ACCIDENTAL

SERIOUSNESS

MILD · MODERATE · SEVERE

FREQUENCY

- Very Common **5**
- Common **4**
- Uncommon **3**
- Rare **2**
- Very Rare **1**

PROGNOSIS

GUARDED · POOR · FAIR · GOOD · EXCELLENT

AGE AFFECTED (MONTHS):

0 — 1 — 2 — 3 — 4 — 5 — 6 — 7 — 8 — 9 — 10 — 11 — 12

BREEDS MOST COMMONLY AFFECTED:

Golden Retrievers, American Cocker Spaniels, Poodles, Bedlington Terriers, and Samoyeds

Clinical Signs

Mild

- Excessive tearing
- Tear staining down the face (orange/brown)

Diagnosis

A veterinarian will perform an examination on the eye to see if he can see the tear duct. Sometimes, they are completely closed over and not obvious. A simple test can be performed in the veterinary clinic to determine if the tear duct is open all the way. Some fluorescein stain will be dropped into the eye, and then flushed with water. If the tear ducts are open, the stain will become apparent in the nostrils within one minute.

Treatment

Without surgical correction, the tear duct will remain closed; however, the excessive tears can be managed at home if not extreme.

Home Management

Daily cleaning with cooled boiled water of the areas where the tears are falling down the face will help keep the eyes clean. Tears are not just water; they contain mucus too. So, if allowed to accumulate, it can cause some irritation to the skin, and potentially even a skin infection. Cleaning will help avoid this.

Surgical Management

Blocked tear ducts can be corrected with surgery. Firstly, if the duct looks partially open, the veterinarian will try to flush through it with a catheter and high-pressure saline. If that is unsuccessful, or the opening is completely closed, the tear duct can be cut into to open it up. Afterwards, a tube inserted into the tear duct will prevent it from closing again as it heals. This surgery is usually very effective.

Prognosis

Blocked tear ducts are not usually uncomfortable, and so your puppy will not be suffering as a result of it. With surgical correction, the prognosis is excellent, and there shouldn't be any future problems with the tear ducts.

Brachycephalic Syndrome

About the Condition

The term brachycephalic means 'short-headed,' and dogs which are brachycephalic can have obstructive breathing issues because of the shape of their anatomy. Not all brachycephalic dogs suffer from brachycephalic syndrome, but among certain breeds, it is very common.

Brachycephalic syndrome usually arises due to three different abnormalities in the anatomy; an elongated soft palate in the roof of the mouth, stenotic (narrow) nostrils, and everted laryngeal saccules, which are the tissues located just in front of the windpipe, which in this case is pulled over the windpipe opening and obstructs airflow. A combination of these abnormalities leads to difficulty breathing, particularly on inhalation.

Quick Facts

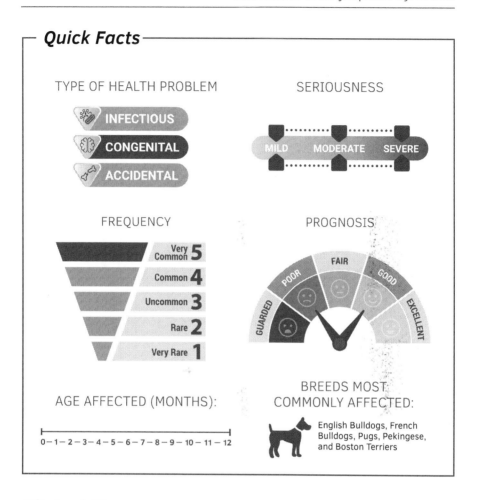

TYPE OF HEALTH PROBLEM

- INFECTIOUS
- CONGENITAL
- ACCIDENTAL

SERIOUSNESS

MILD MODERATE SEVERE

FREQUENCY

- Very Common 5
- Common 4
- Uncommon 3
- Rare 2
- Very Rare 1

PROGNOSIS

GUARDED POOR FAIR GOOD EXCELLENT

AGE AFFECTED (MONTHS):

0 — 1 — 2 — 3 — 4 — 5 — 6 — 7 — 8 — 9 — 10 — 11 — 12

BREEDS MOST COMMONLY AFFECTED:

English Bulldogs, French Bulldogs, Pugs, Pekingese, and Boston Terriers

Clinical Signs

Mild

- Noisy breathing
- Snoring
- Preference for sleeping on their back

Moderate

- Gagging
- Exercise intolerance
- Heat intolerance

Severe

- Blue tongue or gums (cyanosis)
- Difficulty breathing

Diagnosis

It is easy for a veterinarian to diagnose narrowed nostrils by a simple examination; however, diagnosis of an elongated soft palate or everted laryngeal saccules requires your dog to be sedated or under anesthesia. Once sedated, the tongue can be depressed and the back of the throat examined. The tip of the soft palate, and sometimes the larynx, might be swollen, and the soft palate often extends very close to the opening of the windpipe.

Treatment

The only option for brachycephalic syndrome is surgery.

Surgical Management

Elongated soft palates should always be operated on to shorten them, as they can lead to life-threatening obstructions. The laryngeal saccules can be removed at the same time if deemed necessary.

Correction of the narrowed nostrils can be done at the same surgery, or can be performed when your dog is being neutered. This is a simple surgery which opens up the entrance to the nostrils by a small resection of the tissue and a couple of stitches.

Prognosis

Surgery can have some complications, such as post-operative swelling and coughing. But in most cases, this resolves quickly. If the surgery is performed when your puppy is still young, the prognosis is good, and he will be able to breathe with much more ease throughout his life. If the surgery is only performed later in life, the prognosis is less favorable, as damage to the larynx has already been done.

Treatment

Depending on the severity of the damage, treatment may require a visit to the vet or might be able to be managed at home.

Home Management

If the claw is still firmly attached and not hanging loose, a damaged claw can be managed at home. If it is bleeding, simply apply pressure to it for five minutes using a cotton pad. Once it has stopped bleeding, use an ice pack on the area for five minutes, twice daily, to bring down the inflammation and pain.

Keeping your puppy's claws cut short (but not so short that the quick becomes damaged) will prevent the claws from getting caught and causing future injuries.

Medical Management

If your puppy is very sensitive, or has damaged the claw quite badly, he might need pain relief from your veterinarian, and a bandage to stop him from licking the claw.

Surgical Management

If the claw is hanging loose, your veterinarian might suggest surgery to remove the claw. This is done under general anesthetic because there are many nerves in the nail bed, which makes it very sore. Once anesthetized, the vet will remove the nail by using gentle traction, then bandage the paw afterwards.

Prognosis

While claw injuries are uncomfortable, your puppy has an excellent prognosis to make a full recovery.

Cleft Palate

About the Condition

Cleft palates are usually evident at birth, where the two sides of the hard palate, and sometimes soft palate, in the roof of the mouth have failed to fuse. It sometimes goes hand in hand with other facial abnormalities.

It is a serious condition, which leads to difficulty nursing, and inhalation of milk into the lungs. As a result, newborn puppies with cleft palates are often euthanized or die early in life.

Quick Facts

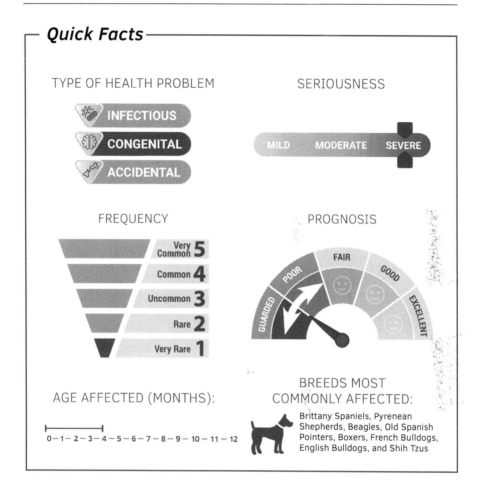

TYPE OF HEALTH PROBLEM

INFECTIOUS
CONGENITAL
ACCIDENTAL

SERIOUSNESS

MILD MODERATE **SEVERE**

FREQUENCY

Very Common **5**
Common **4**
Uncommon **3**
Rare **2**
Very Rare **1**

PROGNOSIS

FAIR
POOR
GOOD
GUARDED
EXCELLENT

AGE AFFECTED (MONTHS):

0 — 1 — 2 — 3 — 4 — 5 — 6 — 7 — 8 — 9 — 10 — 11 — 12

BREEDS MOST COMMONLY AFFECTED:

Brittany Spaniels, Pyrenean Shepherds, Beagles, Old Spanish Pointers, Boxers, French Bulldogs, English Bulldogs, and Shih Tzus

Clinical Signs

Severe

- Food coming out of the nose
- Coughing
- Difficulty breathing

Diagnosis

By examining the roof of the mouth, it is quickly evident whether your puppy has a cleft palate.

Treatment

If euthanasia was not elected at birth, medical management of the cleft palate can be done until your puppy is old enough for surgery.

Medical Management

Since it is difficult for a puppy with a cleft palate to swallow milk, feeding is done through passing a tube into the stomach. This is called orogastric intubation and should be done until the puppy can handle dry dog pellets. If there are any signs of aspiration pneumonia, swift treatment with antibiotics is vital.

Surgical Management

Surgical correction of the soft palate can be performed from 12 weeks of age. The technique will depend on the size of the defect and the location, but most commonly flaps of tissue are used to cover the hole.

Prognosis

Unfortunately, the prognosis for a puppy with a cleft palate is not good, even with surgery. There is a high failure rate, due to the continued growth of the puppy and continuous irritation of the area which has been operated on by food.

Treatment

Home Management

Home management should always go hand in hand with medical management. The area around the eye should be cleaned of discharge several times a day, with cooled boiled water. This will prevent the surrounding skin from getting infected.

Medical Management

Conjunctivitis can be treated with medicated eye drops to soothe the eye and fight any infection. These also heal up trauma quicker than if it was left untreated.

Prognosis

Eyes heal very quickly, and most conjunctivitis cases will resolve within five days of medical treatment.

drawer test, and a tibial thrust test. These can be done on a conscious dog, but if your dog is in particular pain, the vet may decide to sedate him.

X-rays are commonly also performed to ensure there is no damage to other structures of the stifle joint, and sometimes arthroscopy is performed, whereby a camera is placed into the joint to assess for further internal damage to other structures such as the meniscus.

Treatment

Treatments can include medical and surgical therapies. Surgery is the gold standard, and will ensure the quickest return to function, but it is more invasive and expensive than medical management. As a result, each dog is assessed on a case by case basis.

Home Management

There is a lot which can be done from home to assist your dog with full recovery from a CCL injury. Strict rest is very important, which is often best carried out in a crate. The length of rest will vary depending on the severity of the injury, but may require between two and six weeks.

Weight management is also vital. Excessive body weight pushing down on the injured joint can cause major discomfort and slow down the healing. Therefore, putting your dog on a diet if he needs to shed some extra pounds will help his recovery greatly.

Medical Management

Non-steroidal anti-inflammatories are always used in conjunction with home or surgical management. These will decrease the pain and inflammation in the joint.

Surgical Management

There are several surgical techniques which can be performed, depending on the level of expertise of the surgeon. They are categorized into extracapsular (external to the joint) and intracapsular (inside the joint) techniques. Because extracapsular techniques don't go into the joint capsule, there is less chance of post-operative infections and degenerative joint disease. Intracapsular techniques are more invasive, since the joint is opened up, and are usually performed by a veterinary orthopedic surgeon. These are usually performed for severe injuries, or where it is suspected that the meniscus inside the joint is also damaged.

Prognosis

Following surgical repair, the prognosis for full recovery is good to excellent, whereas conservative management may only provide a fair to good recovery, as there is a higher chance of osteoarthritis development.

If one cruciate ligament has been injured, there is also a higher risk that the CCL will rupture in the other back leg in the next few years.

Diarrhea

About the Condition

Diarrhea is commonly characterized by loose stools, ranging from a little softer than usual, all the way to the consistency of water. The causes of diarrhea can be many, and depending on the cause, the severity may be mild to life threatening.

Diarrhea occurs when the gut lining is too inflamed to absorb water and nutrients adequately into the body. It might be inflamed from an infection, such as bacteria or parasites, or inflammation could be due to dietary hypersensitivities, allergies and stress.

Puppies are particularly prone to diarrhea, especially when they go to their new homes at around eight to twelve weeks of age. In many cases, this is just because they are put through more stress than usual, coupled with a change in diet. However, in some cases, it is because their immune systems are still very immature, and they are now coming into contact with infectious pathogens which they haven't encountered before such as Campylobacter, E. coli, Coccidia, Giardia, Salmonella, Cryptosporidium, Roundworms, Tapeworms, Parvovirus and Coronavirus.

Quick Facts

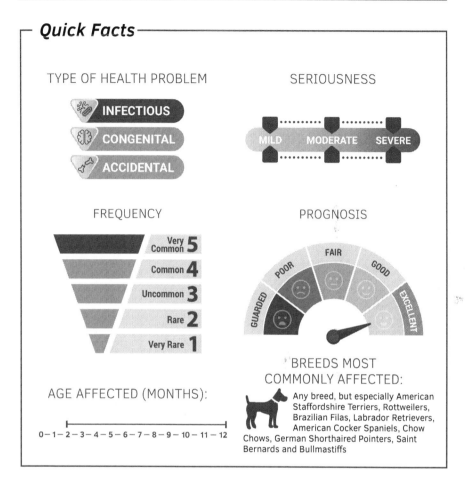

TYPE OF HEALTH PROBLEM

INFECTIOUS

CONGENITAL

ACCIDENTAL

SERIOUSNESS

MILD   MODERATE   SEVERE

FREQUENCY

Very Common **5**
Common **4**
Uncommon **3**
Rare **2**
Very Rare **1**

AGE AFFECTED (MONTHS):

0 — 1 — 2 — 3 — 4 — 5 — 6 — 7 — 8 — 9 — 10 — 11 — 12

PROGNOSIS

POOR   FAIR   GOOD

GUARDED   EXCELLENT

BREEDS MOST
COMMONLY AFFECTED:

Any breed, but especially American Staffordshire Terriers, Rottweilers, Brazilian Filas, Labrador Retrievers, American Cocker Spaniels, Chow Chows, German Shorthaired Pointers, Saint Bernards and Bullmastiffs

Clinical Signs

Mild

• Diarrhea

Moderate

• Vomiting
• Weight Loss
• Decreased appetite

Severe

• Lethargy
• Dehydration

Diagnosis

All puppies with diarrhea must be checked over by a vet. Puppies can fade very fast if they are not absorbing the adequate nutrition and hydration that they need, and so the root cause should always be investigated.

Your vet will start with taking a clinical history and performing an examination, which includes taking a temperature and feeling the puppy's abdomen. He may also take X-rays or ultrasound scans to look at the abdominal organs.

The most definitive way of diagnosing the cause of diarrhea is with a stool sample. Three consecutive days of stools should be submitted to the laboratory for diagnosis, as some infectious pathogens are only excreted intermittently.

Treatment

Diarrhea is usually treated medically alongside good home care.

Home Management

Your puppy should be fasted for 12-24 hours on the advice of your vet, to give his intestines a rest. The younger the puppy, the shorter the fasting time, as puppies struggle to maintain their blood glucose levels for long periods of starvation.

Following the period of fasting, a bland diet should be fed until the diarrhea has resolved. This can be a home-cooked diet of boiled, skinless chicken breast and rice, or you can purchase a gastrointestinal diet from your local veterinarian.

Medical Management

Medical management will depend on the cause and severity of the diarrhea. If your puppy is very dehydrated, he may need intravenous fluids. If he is still bright and bouncing around, he may be sent home with a probiotic, and a fecal binder paste, to soothe the intestines and slow down the loss of water. De-wormers are also commonly prescribed. Antibiotics are also sometimes prescribed by a veterinarian; however, there is now a lot of evidence suggesting that antibiotics are not very effective against gastrointestinal infections, and should not be prescribed as a first line treatment.

Prognosis

Most dogs recover from diarrhea within a few days without lasting consequences.

Diagnosis

Diagnosis of distemper can be done at a laboratory using a sample of blood, urine, bone marrow or discharge from the eyes, airways or reproductive tract. Your veterinarian will take samples and send them off to a lab.

Treatment

Treatment is aimed at supporting your puppy's vital organs and limiting secondary bacterial infections. If your puppy has distemper, he will need to be hospitalized for intensive medical treatment.

Medical Management

If your puppy has distemper and is hospitalized, the veterinarian is likely to give him antibiotics, to stop secondary infections, provide intravenous fluids, use medications such as pain relief, anti-convulsants and medication to bring down a fever, and provide excellent nursing care, which may include tube feeding.

Prognosis

Unfortunately, treatment of distemper when neurological signs are evident is often unsuccessful. If there are no neurological signs, there is a better prognosis with swift, aggressive care, but it is a serious disease with tragic consequences.

ine them under the microscope. This allows him to easily differentiate between the different types of infections.

For very bad infections, or ones which do not respond to treatment, sterile swab samples may be taken and sent to the laboratory for analysis. A bacterial culture can then be performed so that different types of antibiotics can be tested to see what is most effective.

Treatment

Despite there being many 'home remedies' for ear infections that may or may not work, it is best to seek clinical treatment from your veterinarian.

Home Management

Alongside medical management, the ears should be cleansed daily to remove build-up of wax and discharge. This is important, otherwise the medicated ear drops cannot reach the area to be treated.

Many groomers advocate for plucking the ear hair to open up the ear canal and get more oxygen to the lining. While this may help as a preventative measure for ear infections, it should never be done while the ear is sore, as it will exacerbate the inflammation.

Medical Management

Daily medicated ear drops, which can only be dispensed by a veterinarian, will help clear up the infection. These ear drops usually contain a mixture of an antibiotic, an anti-yeast medication and a steroid to reduce the inflammation. If it is a severe infection, oral medication may also be prescribed.

Surgical Management

If the ear canal is completely blocked by discharge, your veterinarian may flush the ear canal with saline under general anesthetic. This then allows him to check that the tympanic membrane is intact and ensure that the infection has not migrated to the middle ear.

Prognosis

Uncommonly, some ear infections can end up being chronic in nature due to bacterial resistance to certain medications. However, most uncomplicated ear infections will clear up within a week with routine ear drops.

Ectopic Ureters

About the Condition

The ureter is the tube running from the kidney to the bladder. An ectopic ureter is a defect where the tube doesn't open up into the bladder, but instead opens up into the urethra, which is the tube running from the bladder to the genitals.

Female dogs are affected eight times more frequently than male dogs, but the incidence is still rare, with 0.016% to 0.045% being affected.

Quick Facts

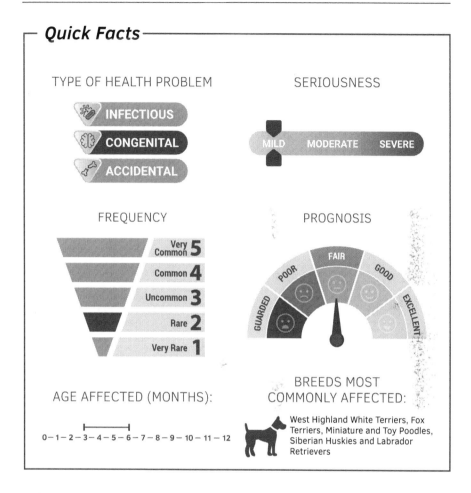

TYPE OF HEALTH PROBLEM

- INFECTIOUS
- CONGENITAL
- ACCIDENTAL

SERIOUSNESS

MILD   MODERATE   SEVERE

FREQUENCY

- Very Common 5
- Common 4
- Uncommon 3
- Rare 2
- Very Rare 1

PROGNOSIS

GUARDED   POOR   FAIR   GOOD   EXCELLENT

AGE AFFECTED (MONTHS):

0 − 1 − 2 − 3 − 4 − 5 − 6 − 7 − 8 − 9 − 10 − 11 − 12

BREEDS MOST COMMONLY AFFECTED:

West Highland White Terriers, Fox Terriers, Miniature and Toy Poodles, Siberian Huskies and Labrador Retrievers

Clinical Signs

Mild

- Inability to naturally void urine
- Leaking urine
- Urine scalding

Diagnosis

A diagnosis of ectopic ureters can be confirmed with a procedure called intravenous urography. This is when intravenous dye is injected, which pools in the kidneys. It then travels to the bladder and out of the body. This dye is radio-opaque, meaning it shows up on X-rays. So, the course of the ureters can be analyzed with X-ray imaging.

Treatment

There are several surgical techniques to treating ectopic ureters, however the success rate is variable.

Medical Management

Medications such as phenylpropanolamine may help to minimize incontinence; however, it will never solve the problem.

Surgical Management

Specialist surgery aims to move the opening of the affected ureters into the bladder so that the urine flows into the bladder to be stored, rather than immediately leaked out through the urethra.

Prognosis

Potential complications of the surgery include continued incontinence, inability to urinate, and a condition called hydronephrosis, where the urine backs up into the kidneys.

Eye Ulcers

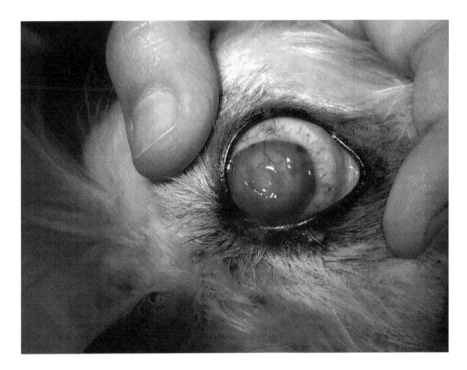

About the Condition

The cornea is the outer layer of your dog's eye. A corneal ulcer is one of the most uncomfortable eye ailments that a dog can experience. Even tiny ulcers can cause great pain. Ulcers can arise for many reasons. The most common reason is because of a traumatic abrasion. This could be from something as big as a stick which your dog's eye contacted on a walk, or as small as a dust particle. Another frequent reason for a corneal ulcer is an object getting stuck in your dog's eye. Grass seeds are foreign bodies that often get stuck under the third eyelid.

Eye ulcers are very common in young dogs, because they excitably explore new things on their walks, which involves putting their head into bushes which can cause trauma.

Quick Facts

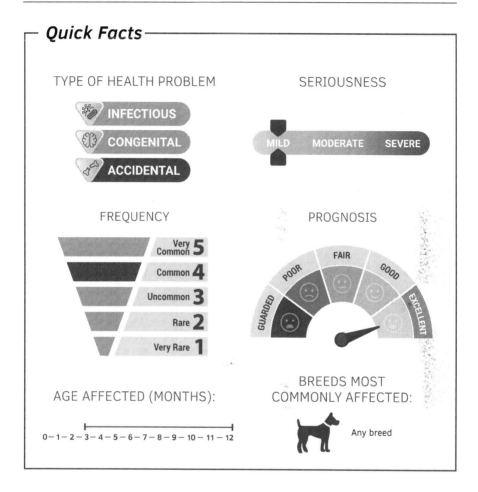

TYPE OF HEALTH PROBLEM

INFECTIOUS
CONGENITAL
ACCIDENTAL

SERIOUSNESS

MILD   MODERATE   SEVERE

FREQUENCY

Very Common 5
Common 4
Uncommon 3
Rare 2
Very Rare 1

PROGNOSIS

POOR   FAIR   GOOD
GUARDED   EXCELLENT

AGE AFFECTED (MONTHS):

0 — 1 — 2 — 3 — 4 — 5 — 6 — 7 — 8 — 9 — 10 — 11 — 12

BREEDS MOST COMMONLY AFFECTED:

Any breed

Clinical Signs

Mild

- Tearing
- Excessive blinking
- Redness of the eye
- Squinting
- Rubbing eye on objects

Diagnosis

Your veterinarian can easily diagnose a corneal ulcer by examining the eye with an ophthalmoscope to check both the inside and the outside. A fluorescein stain will then be dropped into the eye and flushed out with water. This adheres to the damaged layer of the cornea and shows any trauma when a blue light is shone on it.

Treatment

Most eye ulcers will heal by themselves over the course of a few days, but medication should always be prescribed from your vet to avoid the ulcer becoming infected, and also speed up the rate of healing since it is so painful.

Medical Management

Most eye ulcers will heal with broad-spectrum antibiotic eye drops. This helps lubricate the eye, speeds up healing and stops an infection from worsening. Your vet may also prescribe drops which help the collagen to repair the damage quicker.

In rare cases where the eyedrops do not heal up the ulcer, platelet-rich plasma drops can be made from the blood of your dog. These are anti-inflammatory and promote healing.

Prognosis

Eyes both deteriorate and heal very fast. A normal eye, with no underlying conditions, will heal at a rate of 1-2mm per day. So, an ulcer which is 4mm across will only take a few days to heal.

Treatment

Eyelid deformities can only be treated with surgery; however, they can be managed at home and with medications from your veterinarian.

Home Management

Since the deformities often lead to excessive tearing, wiping away the tears with some cooled, boiled water and a cotton pad twice a day, will help keep the skin clean and free from secondary infections.

Medical Management

If the eyelid deformity leads to corneal ulceration or conjunctivitis, your veterinarian will prescribe some medicated eyedrops to help heal the eye.

Surgical Management

Surgical correction of the deformity can be done from about six months of age, and may be corrected at the time of neutering; however, if the problem is not impacting your puppy's welfare, your veterinarian may choose to wait until your puppy is fully grown to avoid needing a second surgery as he continues to grow.

Prognosis

With surgical correction, the deformity will be completely cured and the eye will be comfortable again.

Treatment

Home Management

Once it's confirmed that the diet is the issue, and not an infection, swapping back to the original food for a few days should resolve the problem. Once your puppy's stomach is no longer sensitive, transitioning slowly to the new diet, over the course of one to two weeks, will help his gastrointestinal system acclimatize to the new food.

Medical Management

If the diarrhea is very loose, your veterinarian may prescribe a fecal binder to stop your puppy from losing too much fluid. This is usually a paste which is also combined with probiotics, and kaolin, to decrease the inflammation in the lining of the intestines.

Prognosis

Most puppies are never actually ill with food sensitivities, and once they are transitioned gradually onto a new diet, there are unlikely to be any ongoing problems.

Gastrointestinal Foreign Bodies and Obstructions

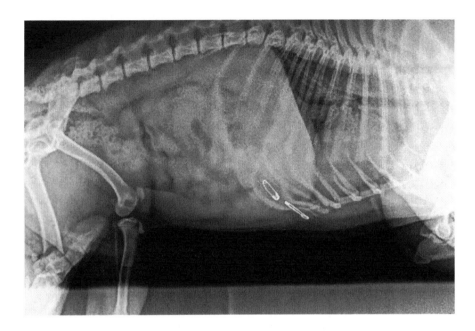

About the Condition

When you bring your puppy home from the breeder, he is inevitably going to want to explore everything in his new environment. Alongside that, throughout the first year of life, puppies lose their baby teeth and grow their adult teeth. This causes their gums to be itchy. The drive to explore, coupled with the need to relieve the discomfort of his gums, means that everything will end up in the mouth of your puppy!

Some puppies will simply chew an object and spit it out again, but there is a risk of swallowing these objects. A foreign body in the gastrointestinal system, especially in a small puppy, can be very serious if it forms an obstruction. Some foreign bodies may be able to pass naturally, and your vet is the best person to make a judgment on that. There may be other risks with foreign bodies as well, depending on the object. For example, sharp objects may cause intestinal lacerations, and batteries can lead to acid burns.

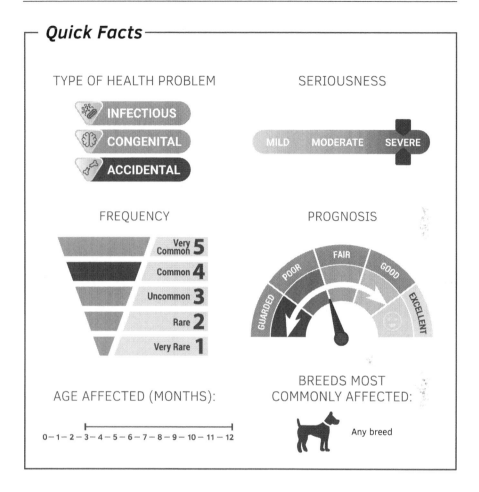

Quick Facts

TYPE OF HEALTH PROBLEM

INFECTIOUS

CONGENITAL

ACCIDENTAL

SERIOUSNESS

MILD   MODERATE   SEVERE

FREQUENCY

Very Common 5
Common 4
Uncommon 3
Rare 2
Very Rare 1

PROGNOSIS

GUARDED   POOR   FAIR   GOOD   EXCELLENT

AGE AFFECTED (MONTHS):

0 — 1 — 2 — 3 — 4 — 5 — 6 — 7 — 8 — 9 — 10 — 11 — 12

BREEDS MOST COMMONLY AFFECTED:

Any breed

Clinical Signs

Severe

- Abdominal pain
- Vomiting
- No stools being passed
- Not eating
- Lethargic
- Groaning

Diagnosis

If your vet suspects a foreign body obstruction, he will start by palpating the puppy's abdomen. Sometimes obstructions can be physically felt. Next, diagnostic imaging is likely to be used to confirm where the foreign body is and how big it is. X-rays are best for this, although sometimes ultrasound scans may also be performed.

If your vet feels that the foreign body may pass naturally, he may perform a contrast X-ray, where he will feed your puppy a barium meal, and take sequential X-rays over the course of the following few hours. The barium shows up as bright white on an X-ray, and will be able to indicate whether anything can pass the foreign body, and whether it is moving through the digestive tract by itself.

Treatment

Foreign body ingestion should be treated as an emergency. A puppy can rapidly die from an obstruction, so it should be treated as soon as possible.

Surgical Management

If a foreign body has been confirmed on X-ray and is too big to pass naturally, the only treatment option is to surgically remove it. The risk of surgery can vary, depending on how long the foreign body has been inside the puppy, whether it is in the stomach or intestine, and whether the surrounding stomach or intestine is still healthy.

Prognosis

If identified and operated on early, the prognosis after foreign body ingestion can be good. However, if the intestine has perforated, and the abdomen has become septic, the prognosis can be poor or guarded, as this is a life-threatening condition.

Heart Murmurs

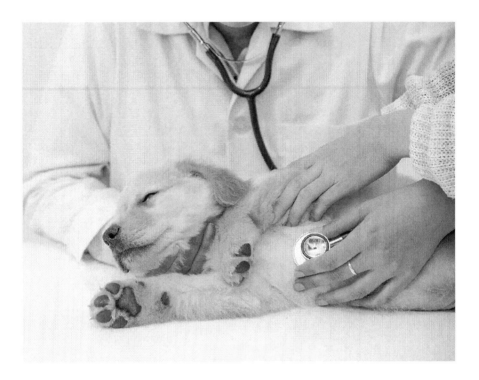

About the Condition

A heart murmur is a sound that can be heard with a stethoscope when listening to the heart. It occurs when there is a turbulent flow of blood within the heart. Many different anatomical abnormalities can cause turbulent blood flow. Causes of heart murmurs can be congenital, meaning that they are inherited and are present from birth, however they are not common, with less than 1% of the dog population being born with heart murmurs.

The most common abnormalities which cause a heart murmur from birth are aortic stenosis, pulmonic stenosis and patent ductus arteriosus (PDA). Less commonly, there can be septal defects, which is when there is a hole in the middle of the heart adjoining the two sides.

If your puppy has a murmur, you should not immediately panic, as in puppies, murmurs are not always due to a heart defect. Young puppies under 6 months of age can have completely innocent murmurs, which go away with time.

Quick Facts

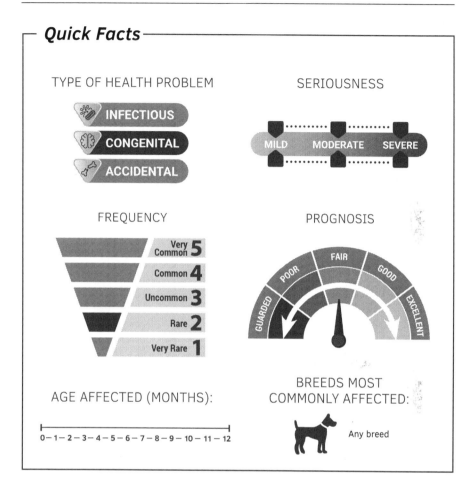

TYPE OF HEALTH PROBLEM

INFECTIOUS

CONGENITAL

ACCIDENTAL

SERIOUSNESS

MILD   MODERATE   SEVERE

FREQUENCY

Very Common **5**
Common **4**
Uncommon **3**
Rare **2**
Very Rare **1**

PROGNOSIS

GUARDED POOR FAIR GOOD EXCELLENT

AGE AFFECTED (MONTHS):

0 — 1 — 2 — 3 — 4 — 5 — 6 — 7 — 8 — 9 — 10 — 11 — 12

BREEDS MOST COMMONLY AFFECTED:

Any breed

Clinical Signs

Mild

- Low grade heart murmur

Moderate

- Slowing down
- Exercise intolerance

Severe

- High grade heart murmur
- Fainting
- Coughing
- Difficulty breathing
- Pale gums

Diagnosis

To diagnose the cause of your puppy's heart murmur, your vet is likely to do a physical examination, electrocardiography (ECG), X-rays or echocardiography (ultrasound scan). These tests will enable your vet to grade how bad the murmur is on a scale of one to six, visualize the anatomy of the heart, and assess how detrimental the heart murmur is.

Treatment

If your vet has determined that the murmur is not an innocent murmur, medication or surgery is likely to be needed to ensure the heart can pump effectively.

Medical Management

Medical management of heart murmurs involves medications which help the heart fill and pump more effectively. This helps decrease the stress on the heart from trying to pump against turbulent blood.

Surgical Management

If the anatomical abnormality in the heart can be fixed, a veterinary cardiologist may opt to do corrective surgery. This is a specialist surgery and will only be done in a referral center.

Prognosis

The prognosis for heart murmurs is highly variable depending on the anatomical cause. Some heart murmurs will cause sudden death, whereas others are mild, and your dog can live a full life without any ill effects.

Heartworm

About the Condition

Heartworm disease is potentially fatal. It is caused by worms which reside in the heart and lungs, causing failure of these organs. Even if treated, there can be lasting damage after an infection, significantly impacting your dog's health. So, prevention is much better than cure.

When heartworms reproduce, the juvenile heartworms, known as microfilaria, circulate around the body in the blood. When a mosquito bites an infected animal, it picks up the microfilaria, which then develop into larvae in the mosquito. The larvae are then transmitted to another dog when that mosquito bites them.

It takes six months for the larvae to develop into adult heartworms, which is why it is uncommon for puppies under the age of six months to have heartworm disease, but that does not mean they don't have the larvae. Therefore, prevention from the age of eight weeks is vital.

Quick Facts

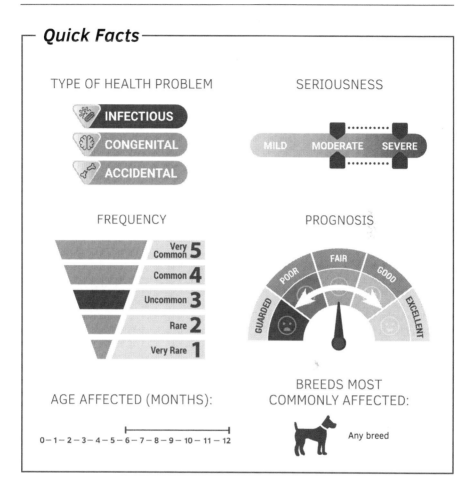

TYPE OF HEALTH PROBLEM

- **INFECTIOUS**
- CONGENITAL
- ACCIDENTAL

SERIOUSNESS

MILD   MODERATE   SEVERE

FREQUENCY

- Very Common **5**
- Common **4**
- Uncommon **3**
- Rare **2**
- Very Rare **1**

PROGNOSIS

GUARDED   POOR   FAIR   GOOD   EXCELLENT

AGE AFFECTED (MONTHS):

0 — 1 — 2 — 3 — 4 — 5 — 6 — 7 — 8 — 9 — 10 — 11 — 12

BREEDS MOST COMMONLY AFFECTED:

Any breed

Clinical Signs

Moderate

- Persistent cough
- Exercise intolerance

Severe

- Lethargy
- Weight loss
- Swollen belly
- Heart attack
- Labored breathing
- Pale gums
- Dark blood-colored urine

Diagnosis

Heartworm testing can be done by a veterinarian, and if you live in a heartworm endemic area it is a good idea to have your dog tested for them every year at his annual checkup. All that is needed is a small sample of blood.

Treatment

Heartworms can only be managed medically, and should be treated as an emergency.

Home Management

If your dog tests positive for heartworms, you should immediately restrict his exercise. Physical exertion will exacerbate the rate at which the worms damage the heart and lungs.

Medical Management

Heartworm prevention can be given monthly to puppies under seven months of age without a heartworm test, whereas puppies over seven months who have not had preventative medicine before should be tested before starting the prevention.

Medical treatment of heartworm disease will start with stabilizing your dog. Once the heart is stable, treatment to kill off the worms can be administered. This can be dangerous but is necessary, as the dead worms can then form an embolus and travel around the body, so your dog must be monitored very closely by your veterinarian.

Prognosis

Generally, dogs with only mild signs have a good success rate from the treatment, but if the infection is severe, there is a high risk of complications and the condition can be fatal.

Hydrocephalus

About the Condition

Hydrocephalus is a serious condition whereby fluid builds up in the brain causing potentially life-threatening neurological symptoms.

The main congenital cause of hydrocephalus is a narrowing or absence of a duct in the middle of the brain called the mesencephalic aqueduct. As a result, cerebrospinal fluid can't flow normally. This defect is most common in toy breed dogs.

The main accidental cause of hydrocephalus is trauma, often during a difficult birth. This causes a bleed on the brain, which in turn leads to adhesions which can obstruct the flow of cerebrospinal fluid. This is most common in brachycephalic (short-nosed) breeds, due to the high chances of difficulties giving birth.

Quick Facts

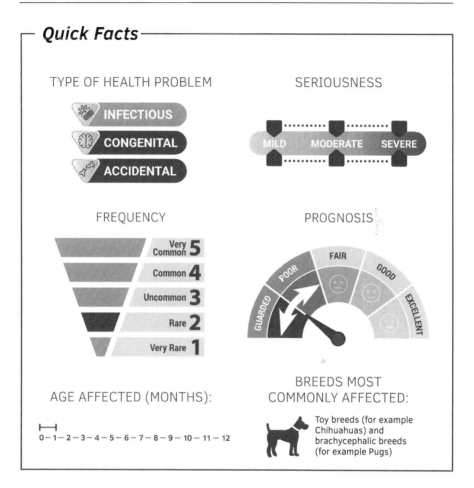

TYPE OF HEALTH PROBLEM

- INFECTIOUS
- CONGENITAL
- ACCIDENTAL

SERIOUSNESS

MILD   MODERATE   SEVERE

FREQUENCY

- Very Common **5**
- Common **4**
- Uncommon **3**
- Rare **2**
- Very Rare **1**

PROGNOSIS

GUARDED · POOR · FAIR · GOOD · EXCELLENT

AGE AFFECTED (MONTHS):

0 — 1 — 2 — 3 — 4 — 5 — 6 — 7 — 8 — 9 — 10 — 11 — 12

BREEDS MOST COMMONLY AFFECTED:

Toy breeds (for example Chihuahuas) and brachycephalic breeds (for example Pugs)

Clinical Signs

Mild

- Asymptomatic

Moderate

- Presence of open fontanelles (holes) in the skull
- Dome shape to the skull

Severe

- Blindness
- Mental dysfunction
- Strabismus – a symptom where the eyes flicker from side to side

Diagnosis

Diagnosis of hydrocephalus can often be made based on a clinical examination alone, however, the root cause of the hydrocephalus should still be pursued. Your vet may not have the imaging technology to carry this out, and a veterinary neurologist might be required to further diagnose the problem. This can be done by ultrasonography through the open fontanelles, CT scan or MRI scan.

Treatment

Treatment of hydrocephalus can be tricky and not always successful, but is aimed at reducing the fluid in the brain.

Medical Management

A veterinary neurologist may prescribe your puppy omeprazole or corticosteroids to reduce the production of cerebrospinal fluid and decrease inflammation.

Surgical Management

If medical management is unsuccessful, brain surgery to shunt the cerebrospinal fluid away from the area where it is accumulating is possible, although high risk.

Prognosis

Unfortunately, the prognosis for hydrocephalus is not very good, as often puppies which are afflicted are still extremely young and weak.

Hypoglycemia

About the Condition

Hypoglycemia is when a newborn puppy has a low blood glucose level. This can be very serious, and if it occurs soon after birth, it is difficult to resuscitate a puppy suffering from it.

Puppies have very few fat reserves and limited ability to generate usable glucose from the food they eat. Therefore, adequate suckling of milk after birth is vital for good health. Too little nursing alone can lead to hypoglycemia, and therefore if the puppy is the runt of the litter and gets pushed out of the way by bigger puppies, hypoglycemia can set in. But there are also other causes. Toxins, septicemia from navel infections, liver shunts and congenital storage abnormalities of glycogen can all cause a puppy to have dangerously low blood glucose levels.

Quick Facts

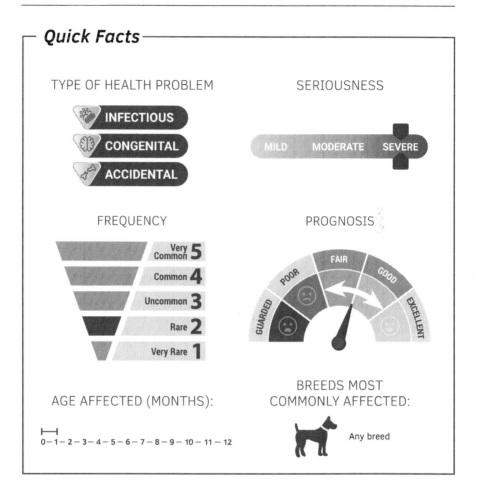

TYPE OF HEALTH PROBLEM

- INFECTIOUS
- CONGENITAL
- ACCIDENTAL

SERIOUSNESS

MILD · MODERATE · SEVERE

FREQUENCY

- Very Common 5
- Common 4
- Uncommon 3
- Rare 2
- Very Rare 1

PROGNOSIS

GUARDED · POOR · FAIR · GOOD · EXCELLENT

AGE AFFECTED (MONTHS):

0 – 1 – 2 – 3 – 4 – 5 – 6 – 7 – 8 – 9 – 10 – 11 – 12

BREEDS MOST COMMONLY AFFECTED:

Any breed

Clinical Signs

Severe

- Lethargy
- Seizures
- Twitching
- Weight loss

Diagnosis

Diagnosis of hypoglycemia is easily done by a vet. Just one drop of blood on a glucometer will measure the blood glucose levels. Normal levels are 80-120 mg/dl (4.4-6.6 mmol/L). Anything below this indicates hypoglycemia.

Treatment

Restoring glucose levels is the most important form of treatment.

Home Management

Puppies should be weighed on a daily basis and supplemented with milk replacement formula to make sure they are receiving adequate nutrition. A normal weight gain is 1–3 g/day/lb. of anticipated adult weight.

Medical Management

If the puppy is a little older and no longer suckling, or is severely hypoglycemic, a veterinarian will need to administer medications to stop any seizures from occurring, and place the puppy on a drip containing glucose, to directly replace the glucose into the blood.

Prognosis

If noticed early enough, most puppies will pull through with dedicated home care.

Intussusception

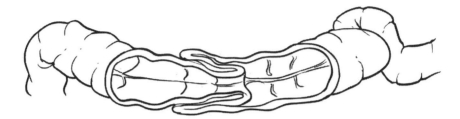

About the Condition

An intussusception is a condition affecting the intestines. It is triggered when the intestines are overactive, such as when there is diarrhea. As a result, a higher part of the intestine envelops the next section of the intestine, causing it to turn inside out.

There are many things which can cause an intussusception including internal parasites, such as worms, parvovirus or foreign body ingestion, all of which puppies are at an increased risk. It can also happen for no known reason; in which case it is known as an idiopathic intussusception.

It can be extremely dangerous, as the inverted section of the intestine will start to die off, and the swelling can result in an intestinal blockage. Intussusceptions are therefore always a surgical emergency.

Quick Facts

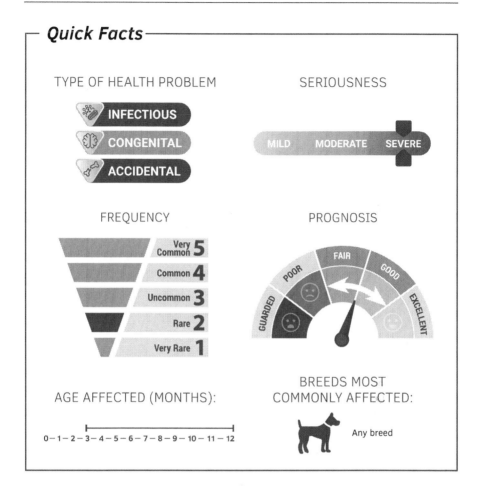

TYPE OF HEALTH PROBLEM

- INFECTIOUS
- CONGENITAL
- ACCIDENTAL

SERIOUSNESS

MILD   MODERATE   SEVERE

FREQUENCY

- Very Common 5
- Common 4
- Uncommon 3
- Rare 2
- Very Rare 1

PROGNOSIS

GUARDED POOR FAIR GOOD EXCELLENT

AGE AFFECTED (MONTHS):

0 — 1 — 2 — 3 — 4 — 5 — 6 — 7 — 8 — 9 — 10 — 11 — 12

BREEDS MOST COMMONLY AFFECTED:

Any breed

Clinical Signs

Severe

- Vomiting
- No stool being passed
- History of diarrhea recently which has now stopped
- Bloating
- Abdominal pain, such as whining, panting, looking at the abdomen

Diagnosis

Your vet might have a suspicion that an intussusception has developed based on the puppy's history and feeling the abdomen, but further imaging is needed to confirm the diagnosis. X-rays can be helpful but imaging is usually done with an ultrasound scan, as there is a typical appearance of a bullseye when scanned in cross-section.

Treatment

Intussusceptions can only be treated surgically and they should be regarded as an emergency.

Surgical Management

The type of surgery done will depend on the health of the intestines. Some intussusceptions can be manually pulled apart, however, if the section of the intestine which was inverted is in very poor health, then it will have to be removed, and the two ends of the intestine will then need to be stitched back together.

Prognosis

If caught early, the prognosis with surgery is good, however if the intussusception has been there several days and the intestine is in poor health, then surgery can be more complicated. In these cases, there is a higher chance of post-operative breakdown of the intestine, which can lead to a septic abdomen. As a result, vigilant post-operative care is vital.

Itchy Skin

About the Condition

Almost certainly, you will see your puppy itch and scratch in the first year of life, and there can be many reasons for this. The most common reason is external parasites, such as fleas and mites. These types of parasites feed off the blood of your puppy, and their bites can cause significant inflammation and itchiness. Parasites can be contracted from the mother even shortly after birth, although since the nervous system of the newborn puppy is still developing, they might not truly start to experience itchiness until they are a couple of weeks old. Parasites can be contracted at any point in your puppy's life, although young dogs are more likely to pick them up than older dogs, because of a higher level of social interaction at places like puppy classes.

Another common cause of itchiness affecting your puppy when you first pick him up from the breeders is the new sensation of a collar. Your puppy won't have worn a collar before, and having something around the neck is an unfamiliar feeling. This will soon pass, and your puppy will get used to it.

Skin infections can also lead to itchy skin, although these are uncommon, as the skin is a natural barrier against bacteria, yeast and fungi. Later in this section, Puppy Strangles will be discussed, which is an uncommon skin infection affecting puppies under 16 weeks old.

Finally, another possible cause for itchiness is allergies. However, allergies usually develop once your puppy has reached a year old, and very rarely develop before 10 months old, and therefore should not be assumed to be the cause of itching in a younger puppy. Allergies can be a reaction to the environment or food, and therefore a process of trial and elimination will help determine the cause. Allergies are usually congenital, and therefore a dog with skin allergies should not be bred.

Quick Facts

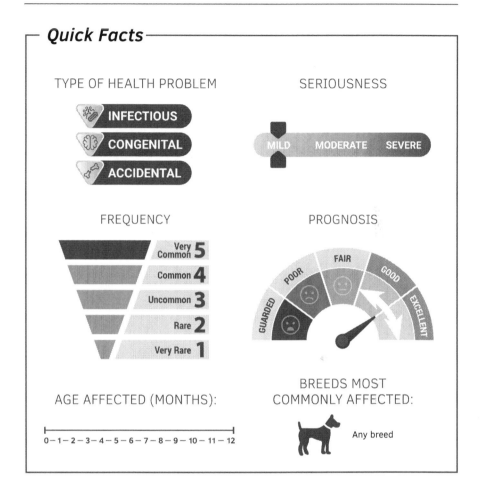

TYPE OF HEALTH PROBLEM

- INFECTIOUS
- CONGENITAL
- ACCIDENTAL

SERIOUSNESS

MILD MODERATE SEVERE

FREQUENCY

- Very Common **5**
- Common **4**
- Uncommon **3**
- Rare **2**
- Very Rare **1**

PROGNOSIS

GUARDED POOR FAIR GOOD EXCELLENT

AGE AFFECTED (MONTHS):

0 – 1 – 2 – 3 – 4 – 5 – 6 – 7 – 8 – 9 – 10 – 11 – 12

BREEDS MOST COMMONLY AFFECTED:

Any breed

Clinical Signs

Mild

- Scratching
- Shaking the head
- Rubbing on furniture or the carpet
- Licking areas of the body

Diagnosis

Your vet may be able to diagnose a skin condition by clinical examination alone. Fleas can be seen with the naked eye, and bacterial infections cause white pimples to appear. However, for some cases where the skin just has a red rash, skin tests may need to be performed to determine the cause. These might include tests such as a skin scrape, hair pluck, tape impression or skin biopsy. Your vet might also take blood to test for mite antigens, or specific allergies if your puppy is older.

Treatment

Itchy skin can be managed in a number of ways, and finding the root cause is imperative for successful treatment.

Home Management

Bathing your puppy with oatmeal shampoo, formulated for itchy skin, will help to soothe the itchiness. If your vet thinks there might be an infection, he might instead prescribe a medicated shampoo which has antiseptic in it. Medicated shampoo must be left on for 5-10 minutes before being washed off, as the longer the contact time, the more effective.

Adding omega oils to your puppy's diet will also help build up the skin barrier, as well as decrease inflammation, as they are natural anti-inflammatories. Your vet probably sells omega oil skin supplements for dogs or can tell you where to get them.

Medical Management

If your puppy is very uncomfortable, your vet might decide to prescribe some tablets, such as steroids or cyclosporine, to decrease the inflammation. Also, if the root cause is an infection with parasites or bacteria, he will be able to provide treatment for that as well.

Skin allergies can also be treated with immunotherapy, where a vaccine is formulated to build up immunity against the allergen. This is not completely effective, but often reduces the discomfort by a considerable amount. However, allergy avoidance is always the key to effective treatment.

Prognosis

Itchiness is never life threatening, but the prognosis depends on the cause. With appropriate treatment, infections will clear up quickly, and have very little residual trouble. Skin allergies, however, are lifelong and impossible to cure, but once they are under control, they can be medically managed with good effect.

Joint Dysplasia

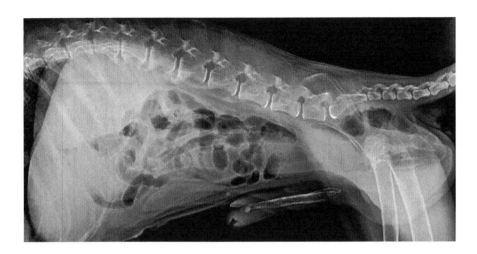

About the Condition

Joint dysplasia of the hip or elbow is a common condition in pedigree breeds of dog. The hip is a ball and socket joint where the head of the femur (ball) fits into a socket in the pelvis. Normally this should be a perfect match, like pieces of a puzzle, but when a dog has hip dysplasia either the ball or the socket is malformed. When the shapes don't match well, it means the joint is less stable when it moves. In several cases of hip dysplasia, the ball can luxate out of the hip socket as it moves, resulting in a wobbly, swaying gait if viewed from behind.

Elbow dysplasia, on the other hand, has many different elements to it. The elbow is not as simple a joint as the hip, and within the elbow dysplasia condition, there can be multiple abnormalities. The most common issue in elbow dysplasia is osteochondrosis dissecans (OCD). This occurs when a flap of joint cartilage separates from the surface. In addition to this, several projections can become detached. These are known as an ununited anconeal process (UAP) and a fragmented medial coronoid process (FMCP). This ultimately leads to lameness or an unusual gait.

Prevention is always better than cure, so buying a puppy from a breeder who has had the parents' joints X-rayed and scored will help you avoid purchasing from poor genetics. Hip and elbow scoring can be done through the British Kennel Club in the UK and PennHIP at the University of Pennsylvania in the USA. The hip score will range from 0 to 106, and the lower the score the better. Each breed has its own median score, which you can look up on the Kennel Club website, and breeding dogs should score below the breed median. Elbow scores measure differently, only ranging from 0 to 3, with 0 being clear, and 3 being badly affected. If the two elbows measure different scores, the worst of the two is listed on the certificate. Breeding dogs should score 0.

Quick Facts

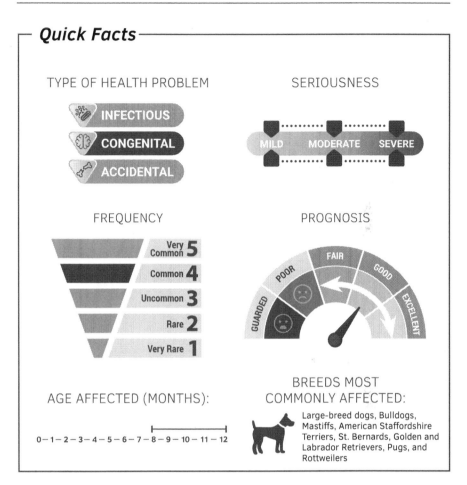

TYPE OF HEALTH PROBLEM

INFECTIOUS

CONGENITAL

ACCIDENTAL

SERIOUSNESS

MILD   MODERATE   SEVERE

FREQUENCY

Very Common **5**

Common **4**

Uncommon **3**

Rare **2**

Very Rare **1**

PROGNOSIS

POOR   FAIR   GOOD

GUARDED   EXCELLENT

AGE AFFECTED (MONTHS):

0 — 1 — 2 — 3 — 4 — 5 — 6 — 7 — 8 — 9 — 10 — 11 — 12

BREEDS MOST COMMONLY AFFECTED:

Large-breed dogs, Bulldogs, Mastiffs, American Staffordshire Terriers, St. Bernards, Golden and Labrador Retrievers, Pugs, and Rottweilers

Clinical Signs

Mild

• Intermittent slight lameness

Moderate

• Constant lameness
• Swaying gait
• 'Bunny-hopping' with back legs

Severe

• Extreme lameness
• Crepitus (creaking) of the joints

Diagnosis

Joint dysplasia is usually diagnosed based on X-rays or arthroscopy (a camera into the joint); however, your veterinarian may have a firm idea that your dog may be suffering from either hip or elbow dysplasia from a clinical exam. Joint dysplasia is an inherited condition which is most obvious when your puppy is almost fully grown, and therefore it is usually diagnosed when your puppy is coming up to his first birthday.

Treatment

Depending on the severity of the joint dysplasia, your vet may recommend managing it conservatively with home and medical management, or opting for surgery.

Home Management

Joint dysplasia can be managed very well with dedicated home care. Keeping your dog lean will reduce the gravitational stress on the joints, and forms a vital part of treatment. Joint supplements containing glucosamine and chondroitin will also help improve the joint cartilage and joint fluid.

Even if your dog wants to be active, keeping walks short and controlled; i.e., on a leash, will prevent extra stress on the joints. He should never be allowed to jump up or out of the car or on or off furniture.

Keeping him fit in other ways, such as with hydrotherapy, will help build up the muscles supporting the joints, as well as provide a fun way to burn off energy which doesn't put stress on the joints.

Medical Management

Alongside excellent home management, pain relief may be needed to help at times when the joints are sore. Your vet will be able to provide the most appropriate medication for your dog.

He may also provide injections of Pentosan Polysulfate, which help to maintain the joint cartilage and prevent it from degrading.

Surgical Management

For severe cases of both elbow and hip dysplasia, surgery is an option to improve the joint. In elbow dysplasia, surgery usually involves removal of bone or cartilage fragments. Sometimes an UAP can be reattached with the use of screws, if surgery is done at a very young age. With hip dysplasia, the hip joint can be modified by removing the head of the femur, reshaping it and replacing it, or taking it out completely. With both hip and elbow dysplasia, total joint replacement is the gold standard surgical treatment, but with implants comes a high cost, as this surgery requires immense skill of the surgeon and expensive implant parts.

Prognosis

With surgery, the prognosis is excellent, as the joint will be fully functional again. Conservative management, however, carries a fair or good prognosis depending on the severity and the dedication of the owners, as the joint will eventually develop early-onset arthritis, due to the abnormal forces placed on it.

Juvenile Vaginitis

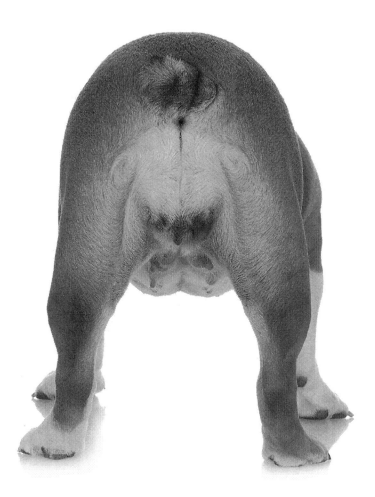

About the Condition

Vaginitis occurs when there is an inflammation of the vagina or vulva in female dogs. It is most commonly seen in prepubertal puppies. Your puppy may have a bacterial infection causing it, which may be secondary to an abnormal conformation of the area, but it can also be caused by vaginal foreign bodies, steroid administration and excessive growth of the vaginal wall.

Quick Facts

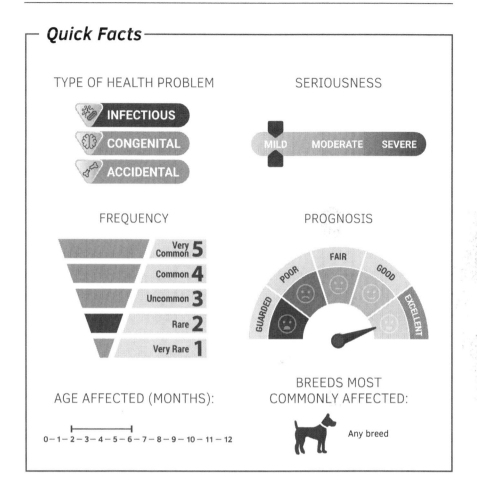

TYPE OF HEALTH PROBLEM

INFECTIOUS
CONGENITAL
ACCIDENTAL

SERIOUSNESS

MILD   MODERATE   SEVERE

FREQUENCY

Very Common **5**
Common **4**
Uncommon **3**
Rare **2**
Very Rare **1**

PROGNOSIS

FAIR
POOR
GOOD
GUARDED
EXCELLENT

AGE AFFECTED (MONTHS):

0 — 1 — 2 — 3 — 4 — 5 — 6 — 7 — 8 — 9 — 10 — 11 — 12

BREEDS MOST COMMONLY AFFECTED:

Any breed

Clinical Signs

Mild

- Discharge
- Licking of the vulva
- Attraction of males
- Frequent urination

Diagnosis

Juvenile vaginitis can be easily confused with a life-threatening infection of the uterus, called a pyometra, however the main difference is that juvenile vaginitis doesn't usually cause your dog to feel unwell, whereas dogs with pyometra will feel very ill. So, even though vaginitis is only a mild health problem, your vet is likely to take it very seriously.

After a clinical examination, your vet may do a blood test to check that your dog is not internally unwell, and perform an ultrasound scan to make sure that the uterus is not infected. Once pyometra has been ruled out, a swab of the vagina should be sent to the laboratory for culture of bacterial growth.

Treatment

Vaginitis can be managed medically, but if it is mild, your vet is likely not to treat it, as it nearly always resolves after the first estrus at the time of puberty.

Medical Management

If there is any foreign material in the vagina, your vet is likely to wash it out, and then prescribe antibiotics based on the culture results of the swab.

Prognosis

Juvenile vaginitis in puppies almost always resolves by itself with the first estrus and doesn't recur again, so the prognosis is excellent.

Kennel Cough

About the Condition

Infectious tracheitis, otherwise more commonly known as Kennel Cough, is a common infectious disease of the trachea, or windpipe.

Kennel Cough is usually caused by a bacteria-virus complex, where two pathogens invade at the same time. These are usually Bordetella bronchiseptica and Parainfluenza. It is most commonly a mild disease which resolves on its own, but in very young or very old animals, it can become extremely serious, or even fatal. Stress and changes in the environment, such as temperature and humidity fluctuations, seem to increase the risks of contracting Kennel Cough.

Kennel Cough is very infectious, so if your dog has Kennel Cough, he should not be allowed to come into contact with any other dogs.

Kennel Cough can be vaccinated against, which will greatly reduce the chances of your dog contracting the disease.

Quick Facts

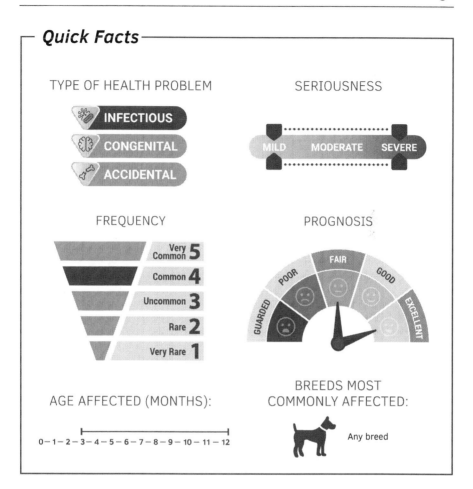

TYPE OF HEALTH PROBLEM

INFECTIOUS
CONGENITAL
ACCIDENTAL

SERIOUSNESS

MILD   MODERATE   SEVERE

FREQUENCY

Very Common **5**
Common **4**
Uncommon **3**
Rare **2**
Very Rare **1**

PROGNOSIS

POOR   FAIR   GOOD
GUARDED   EXCELLENT

AGE AFFECTED (MONTHS):

0 − 1 − 2 − 3 − 4 − 5 − 6 − 7 − 8 − 9 − 10 − 11 − 12

BREEDS MOST COMMONLY AFFECTED:

Any breed

Clinical Signs

Mild

- Harsh, dry cough
- Honking noise when coughing
- Retching and gagging
- Bringing up mucus

Severe

- Pus-containing nasal discharge
- Fever
- Depression
- Inappetence
- Productive cough

Diagnosis

The easiest way to diagnose Kennel Cough is with a tracheal pinch test. This is when your vet will feel the windpipe and apply a gentle pressure, which will elicit a cough. The history and clinical examination will usually be all that is needed for a diagnosis.

In puppies, however, your vet may wish to perform X-rays to determine how severe the disease is, as well as rule out other causes.

Treatment

Since Kennel Cough is usually self-resolving, it can usually be treated from home.

Home Management

Good nursing care is key for recovery from Kennel Cough. Recovery will be sped up by providing your dog with good nutrition and hygiene. Breathing can be improved by making the most of any humid environment, such as taking your dog in the bathroom with you when you shower or run a bath.

Medical Management

Antibiotics are not usually needed to treat Kennel Cough, but if your puppy is particularly young or has Kennel Cough severely, your vet may prescribe them. Cough suppressants may be used to help with persistent coughing, if the cough is non-productive, and medication to reduce the mucus may be used if your dog is frequently bringing up mucus.

Prognosis

Kennel Cough usually lasts for 10-20 days; however, the harsh cough phase is often just for the first five days. For the majority of cases, the prognosis is usually excellent for a full recovery with no residual issues. In young puppies or severe cases, most make a full recovery with swift treatment, however in extremely rare situations, Kennel Cough can be fatal.

Luxating Patella

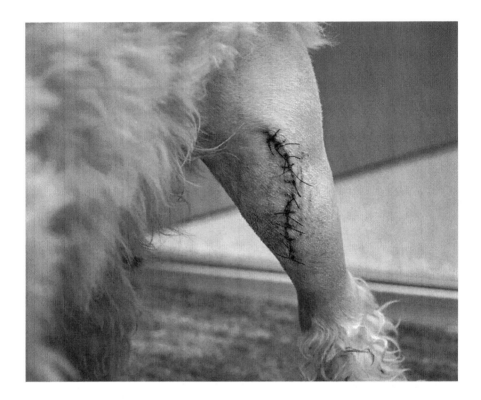

About the Condition

Patella luxation is a very common hereditary condition. The patella is otherwise known as the kneecap. It slides up and down in the trochlear groove, over the stifle joint. When a patella luxates, it slides out of this groove, either to the outside or inside of the leg. In small-breed dogs, it usually slides inwards, and in large breed dogs it usually slides outwards.

When it slides out of the groove, it is not usually painful, but it can cause difficulty with using the leg for a few strides. This is why it is usually recognized through seeing a hop, skip or a lame step.

Patella luxation is measured in severity on a scale of I-IV. Grade I is when the patella can be manually luxated, and slips easily back into place. Grade IV, on the other hand, is when the patella easily luxates on its own, is difficult to return back into the groove, and is associated with significant degenerative processes within the joint. Grade II and III are on a sliding scale in between.

Quick Facts

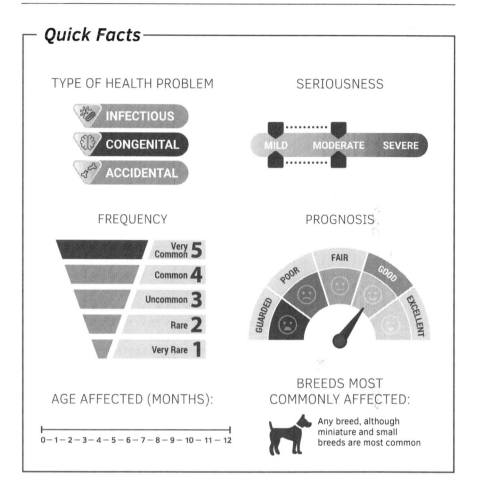

TYPE OF HEALTH PROBLEM

INFECTIOUS
CONGENITAL
ACCIDENTAL

SERIOUSNESS

MILD   MODERATE   SEVERE

FREQUENCY

Very Common 5
Common 4
Uncommon 3
Rare 2
Very Rare 1

PROGNOSIS

GUARDED   POOR   FAIR   GOOD   EXCELLENT

AGE AFFECTED (MONTHS):

0 — 1 — 2 — 3 — 4 — 5 — 6 — 7 — 8 — 9 — 10 — 11 — 12

BREEDS MOST COMMONLY AFFECTED:

Any breed, although miniature and small breeds are most common

Clinical Signs

Mild
- Occasional skipping

Moderate
- Lameness

Diagnosis

A veterinarian can easily diagnose patella luxation by feeling the stifle joint and assessing whether or not the patella moves in and out of the groove. He may wish to take some X-ray images to view the joint, to understand how severe the patella luxation is, and whether it should be managed medically or surgically.

Treatment

There are many options for patella luxation treatment, and it is best for a veterinarian to decide which is the most appropriate, as it will differ from dog to dog.

Home Management

If the patella luxation is not particularly severe, it may be able to be managed at home through keeping your dog's weight under control, and providing joint supplements to support the joint. While gentle exercise is beneficial to build muscle to support the joint, strenuous exercise and jumping should be avoided when managing this condition at home.

Medical Management

Medical management of patella luxation involves pain medications when needed. It will be unusual for a puppy to need medications though, as patella luxation only becomes uncomfortable when the joint degenerates and becomes arthritic. This usually only happens later in life.

Surgical Management

There are many different surgical procedures to correct a luxating patella. If the luxation is a grade III or IV your veterinarian may decide surgery is in the best interests of your puppy, and operate around his first birthday when he is fully grown. Techniques include deepening the groove, suture implants, bone remodeling and Ridgestop™ implants to heighten the edge of the groove.

Prognosis

Prognosis is good in mild or moderately affected animals. They can live a relatively normal life, as long as their joints are cared for through weight management and exercise control.

Malnutrition and Nutritional Deficiencies

About the Condition

With commercial puppy food on the market, it is uncommon for malnutrition or nutritional deficiencies to occur, but there are many advocates, including some breeders, of inappropriate diets for puppies, such as raw food diets. When inexperienced new puppy owners are led to follow these diets without an understanding of their developing dog's nutritional needs, their puppy may suffer.

Nutrition is extremely important for a puppy. Muscles are made out of protein, and growing requires a lot of energy, so if you feed your puppy an adult food, he will not receive the number of calories or amount of protein needed to grow up big and strong. In addition to this, puppies' bones are growing, and they require more calcium and phosphorus than adults. If you don't feed an adequate amount, your puppy may develop brittle bones, or Rickets, leading to pathological fractures and pain.

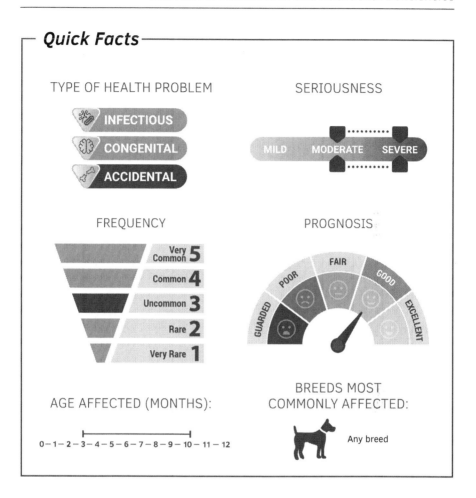

Quick Facts

TYPE OF HEALTH PROBLEM

- INFECTIOUS
- CONGENITAL
- ACCIDENTAL

SERIOUSNESS

MILD   MODERATE   SEVERE

FREQUENCY

- Very Common 5
- Common 4
- Uncommon 3
- Rare 2
- Very Rare 1

PROGNOSIS

GUARDED   POOR   FAIR   GOOD   EXCELLENT

AGE AFFECTED (MONTHS):

0 – 1 – 2 – 3 – 4 – 5 – 6 – 7 – 8 – 9 – 10 – 11 – 12

BREEDS MOST COMMONLY AFFECTED:

Any breed

Clinical Signs

Moderate

- Underweight
- Limping
- Poor muscle development
- Stunted growth

Severe

- Pain
- Stiff walking
- Fractured limbs
- Swollen limbs
- Bowed limbs

Diagnosis

Your veterinarian will suspect a nutritional deficiency based on the history provided to him and a clinical examination of your puppy. He may want to perform X-rays to determine the extent of the problem.

Treatment

You should always follow the treatment recommended by your veterinarian, even if it contradicts the advice of the breeder.

Home Management

An important starting point is to change the diet to an appropriate high-quality commercial puppy food. This will ensure your puppy receives the correct amount of protein, calories, calcium and phosphorus.

If your puppy spends a lot of time inside, taking him outside more frequently to increase his exposure to sunlight will improve his vitamin D levels. This is a vitamin which is involved in bone metabolism.

Prognosis

The prognosis is good, once the diet has been corrected, as long as there are no pathological fractures present.

Mange

About the Condition

Mange is a skin condition caused by mite infestation. Mites can be picked up from the environment or other dogs, and therefore if the mother has mites, the puppies will also get them. The severity of mange varies depending on what type of mites are causing the issue. The most severe type of mange is caused by a mite called Sarcoptes (also known as Scabies mite). Sarcoptic mange can cause such intense itching that a puppy can scratch himself raw in a frenzy. Other mites cause less of a reaction, and some mites, such as Demodex, may never cause any itching at all.

Quick Facts

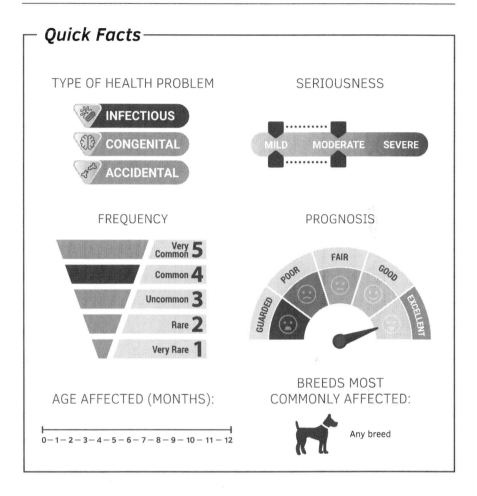

TYPE OF HEALTH PROBLEM

INFECTIOUS

CONGENITAL

ACCIDENTAL

SERIOUSNESS

MILD MODERATE SEVERE

FREQUENCY

Very Common 5

Common 4

Uncommon 3

Rare 2

Very Rare 1

PROGNOSIS

POOR FAIR GOOD

GUARDED EXCELLENT

AGE AFFECTED (MONTHS):

0 — 1 — 2 — 3 — 4 — 5 — 6 — 7 — 8 — 9 — 10 — 11 — 12

BREEDS MOST COMMONLY AFFECTED:

Any breed

Clinical Signs

Mild

• Intermittent scratching

Moderate

• Frequent scratching
• Inappetence
• Red skin
• Open sores

Diagnosis

Your veterinarian may have a strong suspicion that your puppy has mites by just looking at him; however, mites are not usually visible to the naked eye and further tests will be needed to confirm the diagnosis. Tests such as a skin scrape or hair

157

pluck are usually used for diagnosis. The top layer of skin and plucked hair can then be analyzed under the microscope for the presence of mites.

Treatment

Mange can require several months of treatment from your veterinarian.

Home Management

It is important that you treat your dog's environment as well as your dog, as the mites will also live in the areas where he spends most of his time. All bedding and soft furnishings where he lies down, such as the covers of your furniture, should be washed in hot water.

Medical Management

Your veterinarian will dispense three months of anti-parasitic treatment to kill the mites residing on your dog. This is usually in the form of a spot-on pipette or tablet. If this is ineffective, a weekly medicated wash at your vet called Amitraz may be needed to kill off all the mites for good.

Prognosis

Mange can be a major welfare concern, but with dedicated treatment and patience, it can be fully treated with no lasting consequences to your dog.

Neutering-Related Health Issues

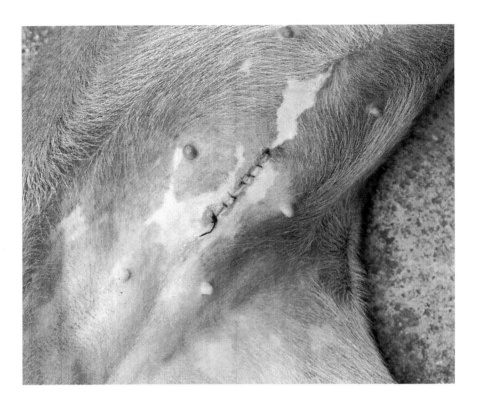

About the Condition

Neutering operations to spay or castrate your female or male dog are likely to happen around six to nine months of age. As discussed in Section 2, general opinion is that the benefits of neutering outweigh the risks; however, after the operation, there can be some health-related consequences. Some of these are related to the operation itself, such as infection, bleeding, seroma formation (fluid buildup under the incision) and opening of the wound if your puppy pulls out his stitches. Other health problems that may be seen later on are related to a lack of reproduction hormones, which include obesity, development of long legs and a risk of orthopedic problems such as cruciate ligament rupture.

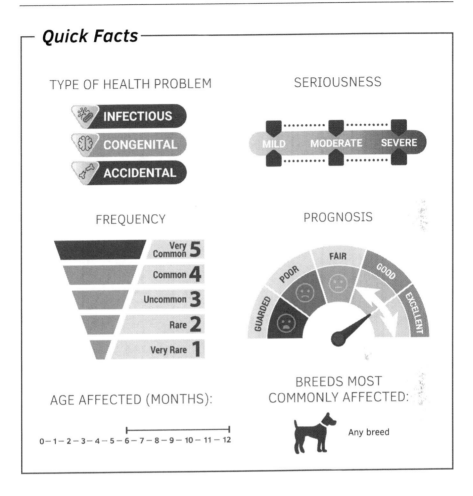

Quick Facts

TYPE OF HEALTH PROBLEM

INFECTIOUS
CONGENITAL
ACCIDENTAL

SERIOUSNESS

MILD   MODERATE   SEVERE

FREQUENCY

Very Common 5
Common 4
Uncommon 3
Rare 2
Very Rare 1

PROGNOSIS

GUARDED   POOR   FAIR   GOOD   EXCELLENT

AGE AFFECTED (MONTHS):

0 — 1 — 2 — 3 — 4 — 5 — 6 — 7 — 8 — 9 — 10 — 11 — 12

BREEDS MOST COMMONLY AFFECTED:

Any breed

Clinical Signs

Mild

- Redness
- Discomfort
- Inflammation
- Scarring

Moderate

- Opening of the wound
- Fluid accumulation under the incision
- Lameness
- Pus discharge from the incision
- Heat
- Bruising

Severe

- Extreme pain such as whining, excessive panting and inability to settle
- Pale gums
- Listlessness

Diagnosis

Your vet will want you to bring your dog back to the veterinary practice to assess his symptoms, especially if they are moderate or severe. Often, a diagnosis can be made based on clinical examination alone, however, an ultrasound examination may need to be carried out to assess the operation site.

Treatment

Your vet's diagnosis will determine how to treat your dog, as some neuter-related health problems are mild and can be managed at home, whereas others can be severe.

Home Management

If your dog's incision site is red and inflamed, or looking swollen, a buster collar to stop him or her from licking the area is vital. You can also place an ice pack wrapped in a towel on the area for 10 minutes twice daily to bring down the inflammation.

Medical Management

Medical management of the post-operative complications is likely to include pain relief, anti-inflammatories and/or antibiotics, depending on the problem.

Surgical Management

In the case of internal bleeding, your vet may need to re-operate to find where the bleeding is coming from. This is likely to be a surgical emergency.

If your dog has pulled out the stitches, he may need to be sedated to re-suture the wound to prevent infection.

Prognosis

Most post-operative neuter-related health problems, if addressed early, will have an excellent prognosis and will heal quickly.

Obesity

About the Condition

Obesity is an under-recognized welfare concern that many dogs battle with. It usually starts in the first year of life, shortly after neutering. This is because reproductive hormones maintain a fast metabolism, and so without them, the weight can pile on. As a result, food portions should be adjusted to avoid this from happening.

While some owners may be unconcerned about obesity, it has many implications on the health of a dog. Excess weight can lead to exacerbation of breathing disorders in brachycephalic (short-nosed) dogs, strain on vital organs such as the liver, heart, kidneys and brain, and also increased gravitational force on joints, which may trigger early-onset arthritis. Thus, it is worth keeping those pounds off your dog.

Quick Facts

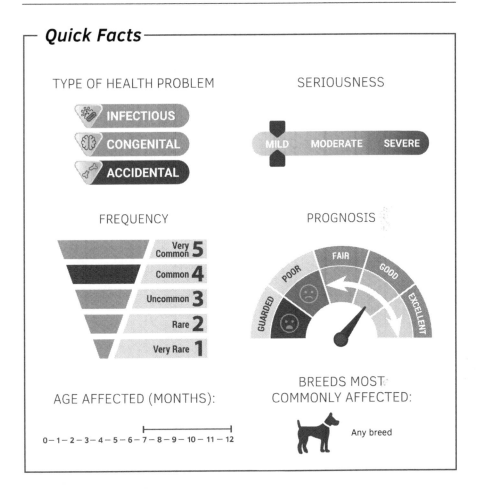

TYPE OF HEALTH PROBLEM

INFECTIOUS

CONGENITAL

ACCIDENTAL

SERIOUSNESS

MILD   MODERATE   SEVERE

FREQUENCY

Very Common **5**

Common **4**

Uncommon **3**

Rare **2**

Very Rare **1**

PROGNOSIS

POOR   FAIR   GOOD

GUARDED   EXCELLENT

AGE AFFECTED (MONTHS):

0 – 1 – 2 – 3 – 4 – 5 – 6 – 7 – 8 – 9 – 10 – 11 – 12

BREEDS MOST COMMONLY AFFECTED:

Any breed

Clinical Signs

Mild

- Body condition score of 6 or more (see diagnosis)
- Difficulty feeling ribs
- No visible waist

Diagnosis

While you can diagnose obesity at home, it is useful to discuss weight management with your vet, as he can help assign a body condition score, so that you know how healthy your dog's weight is. Body condition scoring is a scientific method of scoring a dog's weight, on a scale of one to nine. Four to five is ideal, and body condition scoring helps to set realistic targets to aim for.

1 = Ribs, lumbar back, pelvis and bony prominences are visible from a distance. No body fat. Loss of muscle mass.

2 = Ribs, lumbar back and pelvic bones are easily visible. No fat can be felt. Minimal loss of muscle mass.

3 = Ribs easily felt and may be visible. Tops of lumbar vertebrae visible. Pelvic bones prominent. Obvious waist and abdominal tuck.

4 = Ribs easily felt with minimal fat covering. Waist easily noted when viewed from above. Evident abdominal tuck.

5 = Ribs can be felt without excess covering. Waist observed behind ribs when viewed from above. Abdomen tucked up when viewed from the side.

6 = Ribs can be felt with slight excess of fat. Waist is discernible when viewed from above, but not prominent. Abdominal tuck can be seen.

7 = Ribs can be felt, but with difficulty. Heavy fat cover. Fat deposits over lumbar back and base of tail. Waist absent or barely visible. Some abdominal tuck.

8 = Ribs cannot be felt through heavy fat cover, unless felt with significant pressure. Heavy fat deposits over lumbar back and base of tail. No waist. No abdominal tuck. Some abdominal distension.

9 = Excessive fat deposits over thorax, spine and base of tail. Waist and abdominal tuck absent. Fat deposits on neck and limbs. Obvious abdominal distension.

If your dog has an underactive thyroid, Cushing's disease or is being given corticosteroid tablets, he may be overweight due to medical reasons. Your vet may perform some blood tests in these cases, to see if any adjustment may be made to his medication protocol.

Treatment

Reducing your dog's weight is important for improving his health. There are no options for medical management, such as diet pills, or surgical management, like in humans. Weight loss for dogs requires hard work.

Home Management

The most important place to start is to reduce the number of calories your dog is taking in. It's easy to forget that treats and tidbits also contribute to your dog's daily calories. So, when you measure out how much food your dog should get in a day, remember to subtract some to make up for the calories found in his treats. The packaging of your dog's food will give guidelines on what your dog should be eating over the course of 24 hours. When looking at these guidelines, select the requirement for your dog's target weight, and not his current weight.

Another way to help your dog to lose weight is to increase his exercise. You can increase the length or frequency of his walks, or if he has underlying joint problems such as joint dysplasia, hydrotherapy is also an excellent option. The swimming during hydrotherapy sessions puts zero stress on the joints, and is an excellent alternative form of exercise.

Prognosis

The prognosis for obese dogs can vary from fair to excellent depending on how long they have been obese, and whether they have been able to get back to their ideal weight. On average, overweight dogs live considerably shorter lives than lean dogs, and those that do reach their senior years are more likely to struggle with health implications such as heart problems, liver failure and joint arthritis.

Pancreatitis

About the Condition

The pancreas is an organ which produces enzymes to help digest dietary compo-
nents such as fats, proteins and carbohydrates. Pancreatitis is an inflammation of
this organ due to the enzymes self-digesting the pancreas. Not only is this detrimental to your puppy's health, but it is also extremely painful.

The condition is usually triggered by your puppy eating trash, fatty foods or other
inappropriate foods, such as table scraps. However, for some dogs, there is no apparent reason. Trauma and surgery can also trigger pancreatitis.

Quick Facts

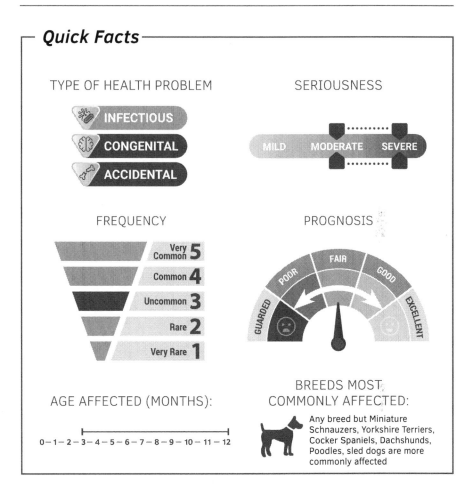

TYPE OF HEALTH PROBLEM

INFECTIOUS
CONGENITAL
ACCIDENTAL

SERIOUSNESS

MILD MODERATE SEVERE

FREQUENCY

Very Common 5
Common 4
Uncommon 3
Rare 2
Very Rare 1

PROGNOSIS

POOR FAIR GOOD
GUARDED EXCELLENT

AGE AFFECTED (MONTHS):

0 – 1 – 2 – 3 – 4 – 5 – 6 – 7 – 8 – 9 – 10 – 11 – 12

BREEDS MOST COMMONLY AFFECTED:

Any breed but Miniature Schnauzers, Yorkshire Terriers, Cocker Spaniels, Dachshunds, Poodles, sled dogs are more commonly affected

Clinical Signs

Moderate

- Loss of appetite
- Diarrhea

Severe

- Vomiting
- Weakness
- Abdominal pain
- Bowing posture
- Excessive panting
- Dehydration

Diagnosis

It is usually possible for your veterinarian to diagnose pancreatitis through a thorough history and clinical examination. A blood test to measure cPLI will give a definitive diagnosis. Your vet may also take abdominal X-rays or perform an ultrasound scan to rule out a foreign body obstruction, as symptoms can be very similar.

Treatment

Pancreatitis is always managed medically, but the severity of the disease will determine whether your puppy can be treated at home or as an inpatient in the veterinary hospital.

Home Management

Dogs affected by pancreatitis should follow a diet that is highly digestible and low in fat, as dietary fat stimulates the pancreas to secrete inflammatory digestive enzymes. There are many commercial and prescription foods available designed specifically for pancreatitis. For many dogs, dietary management alone will keep the condition under control.

Medical Management

Medical management aims to relieve the symptoms and decrease the inflammation of the pancreas. Supportive treatment such as intravenous fluids, strong pain relief and anti-nausea medications are usually the mainstay of treatment. If vomiting is uncontrollable, food may be withheld for a day to give the pancreas a rest.

Prognosis

For most cases of pancreatitis, the prognosis is good or fair, as long as there has been swift action to initiate treatment. In severe cases which have led to organ failure, the prognosis is poorer.

Panosteitis

About the Condition

Panosteitis is a painful condition seen in fast-growing dogs which causes pain in the long bones of the body. It can be likened to growing pains. The exact cause is unknown; however, it has been proposed that stress, infection and autoimmune diseases may play a role. There is also a known genetic link in German Shepherds.

Quick Facts

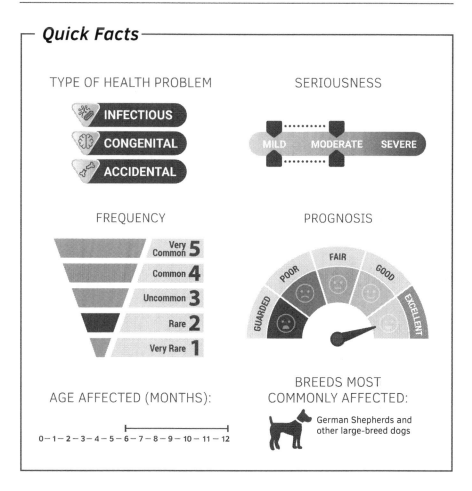

TYPE OF HEALTH PROBLEM

INFECTIOUS
CONGENITAL
ACCIDENTAL

SERIOUSNESS

MILD   MODERATE   SEVERE

FREQUENCY

Very Common 5
Common 4
Uncommon 3
Rare 2
Very Rare 1

PROGNOSIS

GUARDED   POOR   FAIR   GOOD   EXCELLENT

AGE AFFECTED (MONTHS):

0 – 1 – 2 – 3 – 4 – 5 – 6 – 7 – 8 – 9 – 10 – 11 – 12

BREEDS MOST COMMONLY AFFECTED:

German Shepherds and other large-breed dogs

Clinical Signs

Mild

- Limping
- Pain on palpation of the bones

Moderate

- Inappetence
- Fever
- Shifting weight to relieve pain
- Pain in multiple bones

Diagnosis

Your vet will have a strong suspicion of panosteitis based on the clinical exam alone. X-rays are likely to be needed to rule out other causes of lameness.

Treatment

Panosteitis is usually self-resolving by the age of 16 months, so treatment is aimed at relieving discomfort until the disease passes.

Medical Management

Non-steroidal anti-inflammatory and opioid drugs are likely to be the drugs of choice for your dog, to relieve his discomfort during flare-ups.

Prognosis

Once fully grown, panosteitis no longer causes any problems. Even though there are irregularities of the bones during the disease process, they won't be any weaker or underdeveloped in the long run, compared to a dog without panosteitis.

Parvovirus

About the Condition

Parvovirus is a potentially deadly virus which can be picked up from the environment in endemic areas of the world. It is one of the diseases which is included in the core vaccinations which were discussed in Section 2.

Unvaccinated or incompletely vaccinated puppies under six months of age are particularly susceptible to the infection. The virus is shed in the feces and picked up from the environment by dogs lacking immunity, or transmitted by direct contact. It is highly contagious, and resistant to many disinfectants.

The virus destroys the lining of the intestines, and can spread to bone marrow too. Survivors of parvovirus can therefore have lifelong digestive issues.

Quick Facts

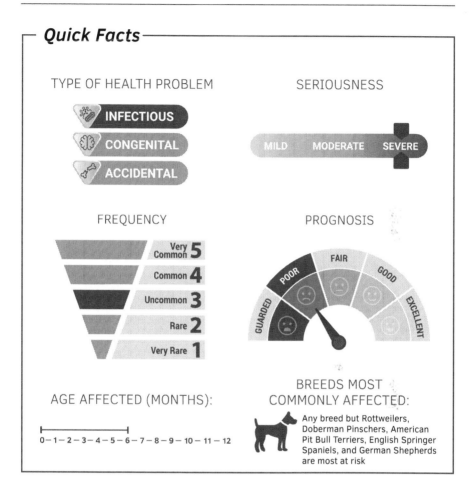

TYPE OF HEALTH PROBLEM

INFECTIOUS
CONGENITAL
ACCIDENTAL

SERIOUSNESS

MILD   MODERATE   SEVERE

FREQUENCY

Very Common **5**
Common **4**
Uncommon **3**
Rare **2**
Very Rare **1**

PROGNOSIS

GUARDED   POOR   FAIR   GOOD   EXCELLENT

AGE AFFECTED (MONTHS):

0 — 1 — 2 — 3 — 4 — 5 — 6 — 7 — 8 — 9 — 10 — 11 — 12

BREEDS MOST COMMONLY AFFECTED:

Any breed but Rottweilers, Doberman Pinschers, American Pit Bull Terriers, English Springer Spaniels, and German Shepherds are most at risk

Clinical Signs

Severe

- Lethargy
- Anorexia
- Fever
- Abdominal pain
- Vomiting
- Hemorrhagic diarrhea

Diagnosis

Diagnosis of parvovirus is quick and simple in most vet practices. There are commercially available tests which give instant results, to ensure puppies with parvovirus get diagnosed early and treated swiftly. A drop of blood, or a rectal swab to pick up feces, is all that is needed. This is then mixed with a solution and dropped on the test strip. The solution runs up the blotting paper, showing one line if it is negative, and two lines if it is positive. If the result is positive, your puppy will need to be immediately isolated.

Treatment

If your puppy has parvovirus, he will need to be hospitalized in isolation to be treated.

Medical Management

Treatment aims to restore lost fluids and electrolytes, and prevent secondary bacterial infection. Intravenous fluid therapy, anti-nausea drugs, anti-diarrhea drugs, antibiotics and electrolytes are usually administered, and if there is significant blood loss in the stools, a blood transfusion may be warranted.

Prognosis

The fatality rate from parvovirus is high; however, if your puppy survives the first three to four days, he is likely to make a full recovery. Complications such as intussusceptions, septicemia, endotoxemia and bacterial infection of intravenous catheters are potential complications. With swift care, between 68% and 92% of puppies recover from parvovirus.

Patent Ductus Arteriosus

About the Condition

When a puppy is still a fetus inside its mother, it doesn't need to breathe. As a result, the lungs are collapsed and not full of air. It is difficult for blood to pass through collapsed lungs as it requires more pressure, so to avoid this, most blood bypasses the lungs through a fetal vessel called the ductus arteriosus, from the right to the left side of the heart.

At birth, the inflation of the lungs makes it much easier for the blood to travel through them, instead of a tiny vessel. As a result, the ductus arteriosus is no longer used and closes to form a ligament called the ligamentum arteriosum.

In dogs which have a patent ductus arteriosus, this vessel remains open. Since the pressure being pumped out of the left side of the heart to the body is now stronger than the right side of the heart to the newly inflated lungs, blood shunts from the left to the right side, causing a volume overload in the heart. This can eventually lead to heart failure.

Quick Facts

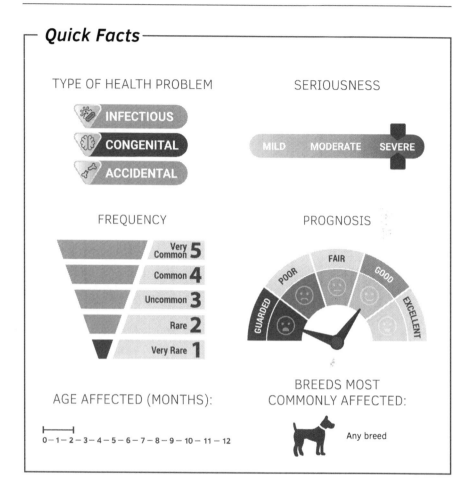

TYPE OF HEALTH PROBLEM

INFECTIOUS
CONGENITAL
ACCIDENTAL

SERIOUSNESS

MILD   MODERATE   SEVERE

FREQUENCY

Very Common 5
Common 4
Uncommon 3
Rare 2
Very Rare 1

PROGNOSIS

GUARDED   POOR   FAIR   GOOD   EXCELLENT

AGE AFFECTED (MONTHS):

0 – 1 – 2 – 3 – 4 – 5 – 6 – 7 – 8 – 9 – 10 – 11 – 12

BREEDS MOST COMMONLY AFFECTED:

Any breed

Clinical Signs

Severe

- Machine-like heart murmur
- Bounding pulses
- Coughing
- Difficulty breathing
- Exercise intolerance
- Fainting

Diagnosis

If your puppy is a newborn with a detectable heart murmur, your vet may wish to adopt a wait and see approach, and listen again to the heart in a few months. This is because sometimes the ductus arteriosus closes by itself within the first few months of life.

If your puppy is already a few months old, and still has a heart murmur, tests such as echocardiography (ultrasound of the heart) and X-rays, will assess the anatomy of the heart and determine whether a patent ductus arteriosus is present.

Treatment

There is a high risk of heart failure early in life for dogs with a patent ductus arteriosus, so surgery is recommended as soon as possible.

Medical Management

Heart failure can be managed medically through the use of drugs which improve the pumping of the heart and reduce the fluid buildup in the lungs with heart failure. However, this just manages the symptoms and is not a cure for a patent ductus arteriosus.

Surgical Management

Surgical closure is the treatment of choice. This requires a veterinary cardiologist to perform the surgery, as operating on the heart is technical and requires specialist equipment. There are two ways this can be done. Firstly, a catheter can be placed in the femoral artery, and advanced to the ductus arteriosus. This is then lodged in place to occlude the vessel. This can be very effective, and is much less invasive than open-chest surgery.

The second surgical technique is to open the chest and visualize the patent ductus arteriosus. A permanent ligature is then placed around the vessel to tie it shut.

Prognosis

With early surgical occlusion of the patent ductus arteriosus, dogs can live a relatively normal, full life. However, without surgical intervention, most dogs will develop heart failure in the first two years of life.

Phobias and Anxiety

About the Condition

Phobias and anxiety are very common in dogs. Puppies are still learning, and look to their mother or owners to understand how to deal with scary situations. The situations that your puppy experiences during his formative early months will set him up for life, or set him back. Since your puppy's behavior is still very malleable when he is very young, phobias and anxiety usually start to become apparent only from approximately six months.

Common phobias include loud noises, traffic, other dogs, other people and being left alone, to name a few. Anxiety is also usually deep-rooted in poor socialization. It is important to work with your vet and behaviorist to help your dog with coping skills while he is still young.

Quick Facts

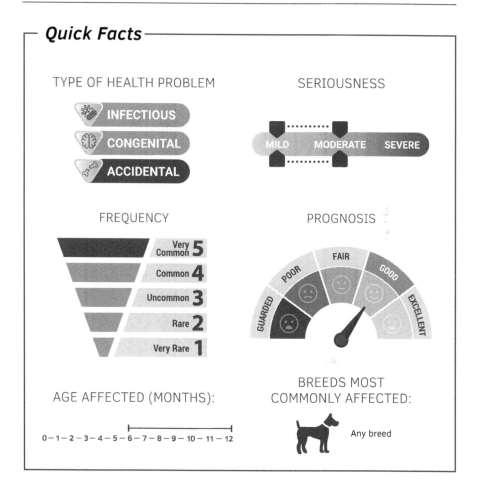

TYPE OF HEALTH PROBLEM

INFECTIOUS
CONGENITAL
ACCIDENTAL

SERIOUSNESS

MILD MODERATE SEVERE

FREQUENCY

Very Common 5
Common 4
Uncommon 3
Rare 2
Very Rare 1

PROGNOSIS

POOR FAIR GOOD
GUARDED EXCELLENT

AGE AFFECTED (MONTHS):

0 − 1 − 2 − 3 − 4 − 5 − 6 − 7 − 8 − 9 − 10 − 11 − 12

BREEDS MOST COMMONLY AFFECTED:

Any breed

Clinical Signs

Mild

- Pacing
- Barking

Moderate

- Aggression
- Inappetence
- Panting
- Destructive behavior

Diagnosis

A veterinarian is not needed to diagnose a phobia or anxiety, as it is likely to be quite obvious to you if your puppy suffers from it. Seeking the opinion of a veterinary behaviorist is often helpful to determine the root cause, severity and how to tackle the behavior.

Treatment

There is no 'one approach fixes all' when it comes to phobias and anxiety. There is a lot you can do for your dog at home, but your veterinarian can also help your dog with anti-anxiety supplements and medication.

Home Management

A behaviorist can work with you in your home to help your dog with any negative feelings he may have. Suggestions might include creating a safe space for him, providing chew toys, as chewing releases endorphins which are relaxing, and staged scenarios, such as leaving the room or house for increasing intervals of time.

For dogs with a fear of storms or fireworks, many owners find that a tight jacket known as a ThunderShirt® can alleviate anxiety. Other dogs appreciate having a den or covered crate to retreat to.

Medical Management

Your veterinarian can provide several options to help with your dog's behavior. Supplements include L-tryptophan, which increases serotonin, the happy drug, in your dog's brain, and casein, which makes your puppy feel like he is suckling from his mother again. Another option is a 'dog-appeasing pheromone.' This can come in the form of a room spray, plug-in adaptor, or wearable collar.

If your dog's anxiety or phobia is particularly extreme, your veterinarian may prescribe a benzodiazepine drug to help him deal with times of heightened stress. This prevents anxiety, sedates the dog, and causes a loss of memory of the stressful situation.

Prognosis

With a combined effort between yourself, you veterinarian and a veterinary behaviorist, it is usually possible to improve your dog's behavior with patience, persistence and positive reinforcement. However, some behaviors are so ingrained that a dog will never fully recover from the anxiety or fear.

Poisons and Toxins

About the Condition

There are many things around the house and in the environment, which can be poisonous or toxic for your puppy. When your puppy is young, he will explore everything around him, so making your house puppy-proof is vital for keeping your puppy safe. This includes keeping household chemicals tidied away; making sure the toilet lid is closed if it has recently had chemicals poured in it; ensuring there are no dangerous objects lying around such as batteries or human medicines; and placing potted plants out of reach. Even certain foods, safe to humans, are toxic to dogs, such as grapes, raisins, onions, garlic, chocolate and chewing gum.

Quick Facts

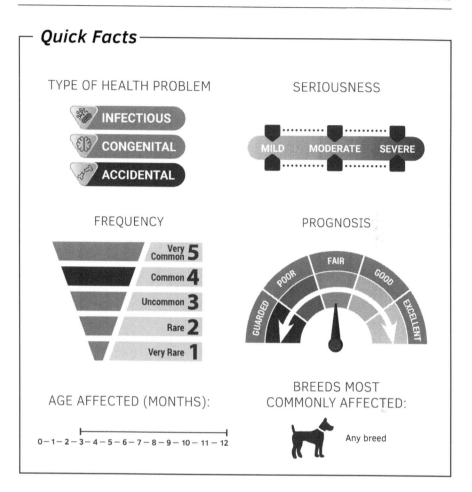

TYPE OF HEALTH PROBLEM

INFECTIOUS
CONGENITAL
ACCIDENTAL

SERIOUSNESS

MILD   MODERATE   SEVERE

FREQUENCY

Very Common 5
Common 4
Uncommon 3
Rare 2
Very Rare 1

PROGNOSIS

GUARDED   POOR   FAIR   GOOD   EXCELLENT

AGE AFFECTED (MONTHS):

0 − 1 − 2 − 3 − 4 − 5 − 6 − 7 − 8 − 9 − 10 − 11 − 12

BREEDS MOST
COMMONLY AFFECTED:

Any breed

Clinical Signs

Mild

- Diarrhea
- Grumbling belly

Moderate

- Vomiting
- Muscle twitching
- Drooling

Severe

- Seizures
- Severe dehydration
- Neurological symptoms
- Unresponsiveness

Diagnosis

Diagnosis of a poisoning is usually based on the history of your puppy eating something he shouldn't have; however, the symptoms can also give an indication that poisoning might be the cause.

Treatment

All potential poisonings should always be seen by a vet immediately, even if there are no symptoms yet.

Medical Management

If the poisonous item has been ingested within the last hour, your vet may choose to try to evacuate the stomach by inducing vomiting. This will remove as many toxins as possible from the body. Following that, activated charcoal will help limit the amount of toxin or poison absorbed into the puppy's system.

If it has been a while since the ingestion, and your puppy is showing symptoms, he will be hospitalized and started on intravenous fluids to flush the toxin out as quickly as possible. He will also be given supportive treatment such as anti-seizure or anti-nausea medications.

Prognosis

The prognosis will vary depending on the type of toxicity. For example, ethylene glycol (antifreeze) toxicity carries an extremely guarded prognosis, whereas ingesting a poisonous plant will usually lead to a full recovery.

Portosystemic Shunt

About the Condition

When a puppy is still a fetus, the liver is not needed. Toxins are filtered in the mother's bloodstream instead. As a result, there are blood vessels present that allow blood to bypass the liver, and meet up with the vena cava; the vein which returns blood to the heart. Towards the end of gestation, these vessels diminish, and blood begins to flow through the liver. A portosystemic shunt occurs when the blood is shunted from the portal (liver) vein, past the liver, and back into the normal vascular system.

Dogs with portosystemic shunts often have other congenital problems too, such as cryptorchidism (retained testicles). Up to 20% of affected dogs have no symptoms at all, but for dogs who are symptomatic, clinical signs will be evident by 1 year of age.

Quick Facts

TYPE OF HEALTH PROBLEM

- INFECTIOUS
- CONGENITAL
- ACCIDENTAL

SERIOUSNESS

MILD   MODERATE   SEVERE

FREQUENCY

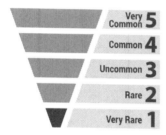

Very Common 5
Common 4
Uncommon 3
Rare 2
Very Rare 1

PROGNOSIS

POOR   FAIR   GOOD
GUARDED   EXCELLENT

AGE AFFECTED (MONTHS):

0 — 1 — 2 — 3 — 4 — 5 — 6 — 7 — 8 — 9 — 10 — 11 — 12

BREEDS MOST COMMONLY AFFECTED:

Yorkshire Terriers, Maltese, Shih Tzu, Havanese, Papillon, Miniature Schnauzers, Pugs, Cairn Terriers, Norfolk Terriers, Tibetan Spaniels, Irish Wolfhounds, Old English Sheepdogs, Labrador Retrievers, and Golden Retrievers

Clinical Signs

Severe

- Nausea
- Vomiting
- Diarrhea
- Pica (eating strange things such as dirt)
- Anorexia
- Drinking more
- Urinating more
- Unexplained blindness
- Vocalization
- Hallucinations
- Neck or spinal pain
- Blood in the urine
- Seizures
- Neurological abnormalities
- Pressing head against walls

Diagnosis

The symptoms for a portosystemic shunt are vague and can resemble many different diseases, so your vet will perform blood tests and X-rays to narrow down the diagnosis. On the X-rays, the liver will look small, and the kidneys may look plump. Vets experienced in ultrasonography may find this useful to diagnose a portosystemic shunt, but it can be easily missed with ultrasound. In a referral hospital, advanced imaging such as CT or MRI scans is useful in determining exactly where the shunt is happening.

Treatment

Surgery is the treatment of choice, but not all dogs may tolerate closure of the shunt, so minimally symptomatic dogs can have a good quality of life with medical management alone.

Medical Management

Medical management for dogs who are not surgical candidates aims to reduce the ammonia in the blood through feeding a prescription diet. This contains only small quantities of very high-quality protein (from which ammonia is derived). Ammonia is the cause of neurological symptoms, and this builds up because the liver is not functioning appropriately to filter it out. Red meat, fish and organ meats must be avoided, and soy and dairy proteins are best. Some vets also prescribe daily lactulose and metronidazole, which are believed to alter the normal bacterial flora in the guts, to decrease the populations of ammonia-producing organisms.

Surgical Management

Surgery to close the shunt requires a specialist soft tissue surgeon as the procedure is complicated. It is likely to be done one of two ways; either the shunt will be ligated with suture material to close the vessel, or an ameroid ring is placed around the vessel which gradually expands over the course of a few days, preventing a sudden increase in blood flow through the liver. A common complication of surgery is an increase in blood pressure, so postoperative dogs must be closely monitored.

Prognosis

There have been a number of studies investigating the survival time for dogs with portosystemic shunts, and they have reported times varying between five and 11 years, for both those surgically and medically managed. Therefore, it is safe to say the prognosis is variable depending on the individual dog.

Puppy Strangles

About the Condition

Puppy strangles is also known as juvenile cellulitis and juvenile pyoderma. It is a relatively rare skin condition of young puppies. The cause is still unknown, although there are different thoughts on the reason for the condition. The most widely accepted explanation is that it is a result of an immune dysfunction. This means the puppy's immune system is attacking the skin.

Quick Facts

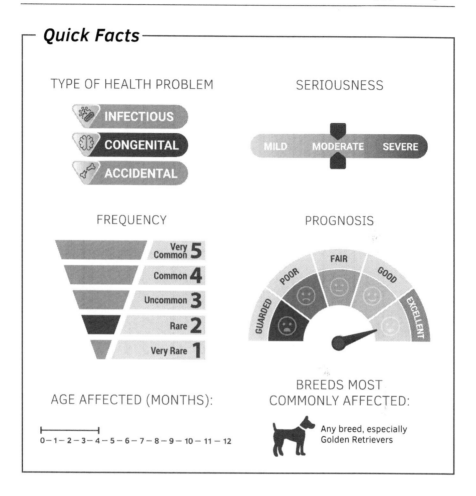

TYPE OF HEALTH PROBLEM

- INFECTIOUS
- CONGENITAL
- ACCIDENTAL

SERIOUSNESS

MILD   MODERATE   SEVERE

FREQUENCY

- Very Common 5
- Common 4
- Uncommon 3
- Rare 2
- Very Rare 1

PROGNOSIS

GUARDED   POOR   FAIR   GOOD   EXCELLENT

AGE AFFECTED (MONTHS):

0 – 1 – 2 – 3 – 4 – 5 – 6 – 7 – 8 – 9 – 10 – 11 – 12

BREEDS MOST COMMONLY AFFECTED:

Any breed, especially Golden Retrievers

Clinical Signs

Moderate

- Swelling of the face and muzzle
- Raised bumps filled with pus, starting on the face and ears, spreading to the body, paws and anus
- Heavy scabbing once the bumps have ruptured
- Swelling under the jaw (lymph node swelling)
- Lethargy
- Loss of appetite
- Fever
- Joint Pain

Diagnosis

There are many conditions which look like puppy strangles, so your vet is likely to run a number of skin tests to rule these out. Skin scrapings will rule out mange, and fungal cultures will rule out ringworm. A skin biopsy might also be performed to look at the skin under the microscope by a pathologist.

Treatment

Both a treatment for the primary puppy strangles, and a treatment to prevent secondary infections is needed.

Medical Management

Since puppy strangles is an immune disease, treatment is based on suppressing the immune system. This is usually done with a steroid, such as prednisone, tapered down over several weeks. This can cause side effects such as increased thirst, urination and appetite.

Antibiotics are also usually administered, as once the bumps rupture, they are open lesions which are susceptible to bacterial infections, especially when the immune system is being suppressed.

Prognosis

Typically, puppy strangles resolves with a couple of weeks of treatment. In severe cases, scarring may remain, but this is only cosmetic.

Retained Deciduous Teeth

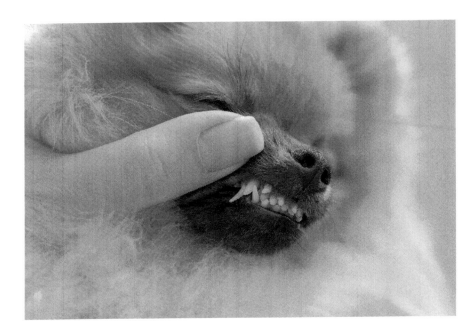

About the Condition

Before the adult teeth come through at roughly one year of age, a puppy's mouth is full of baby teeth, known as deciduous teeth. As the adult teeth begin to erupt, they are supposed to push the deciduous teeth out of their socket. Most owners will never notice their dogs' teeth come out as they will be lost or swallowed, but sometimes they don't come out at all.

When an adult tooth erupts next to a deciduous tooth, the mouth becomes clustered with unnecessary teeth. While this usually doesn't cause much pain for your dog, the deciduous tooth must be removed, as food can easily become impacted in between the teeth and lead to decay and permanent damage to the adult tooth.

Quick Facts

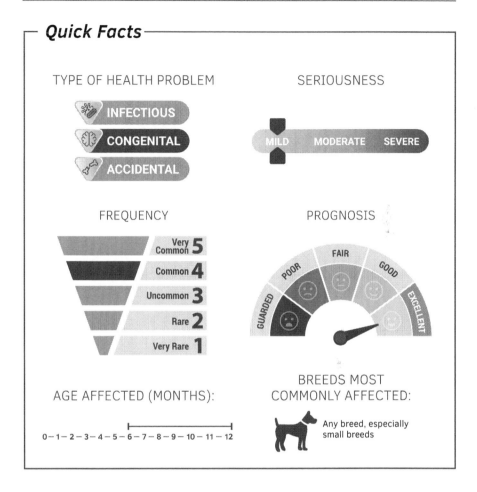

TYPE OF HEALTH PROBLEM

INFECTIOUS

CONGENITAL

ACCIDENTAL

SERIOUSNESS

MILD MODERATE SEVERE

FREQUENCY

Very Common **5**
Common **4**
Uncommon **3**
Rare **2**
Very Rare **1**

PROGNOSIS

POOR FAIR GOOD
GUARDED EXCELLENT

AGE AFFECTED (MONTHS):

0 — 1 — 2 — 3 — 4 — 5 — 6 — 7 — 8 — 9 — 10 — 11 — 12

BREEDS MOST COMMONLY AFFECTED:

Any breed, especially small breeds

Clinical Signs

Mild
- Visible deciduous teeth
- Trapped food
- Dental disease

Diagnosis

Your veterinarian will be able to diagnose retained deciduous teeth with a quick clinical examination of your dog's mouth.

Treatment

If the teeth have not fallen out by your puppy's first birthday, they are unlikely to fall out by themselves, and therefore they should be removed surgically.

Surgical Management

Surgical removal of deciduous teeth is usually a simple procedure as the roots are not very long. It requires a general anesthetic, and your puppy may need some pain relief afterwards for a few days.

Prognosis

As long as the retained deciduous teeth have not caused any major abnormalities in the adult dentition, your puppy will not suffer any consequences once the deciduous teeth have been removed.

Reverse Sneezing

About the Condition

Reverse sneezing is a strange condition which may have you worried when you first see it; however, in most cases it is entirely harmless. The sharp inhalations are caused by a spasm in the soft palate at the roof of the mouth. It is usually triggered by a congenitally long soft palate, but it can also happen for no reason at all. In older dogs, other conditions such as upper respiratory tract polyps can also lead to reverse sneezing, but in puppies, this is very rare.

Quick Facts

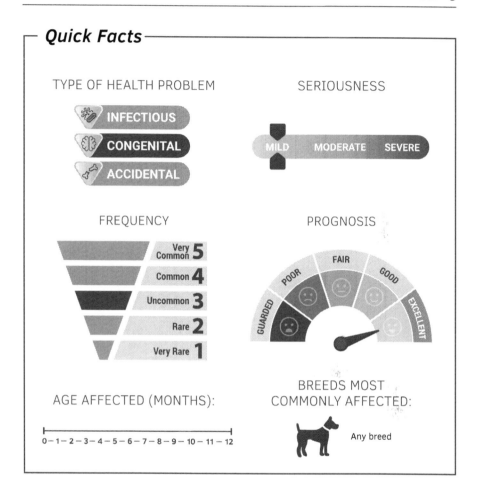

TYPE OF HEALTH PROBLEM

INFECTIOUS
CONGENITAL
ACCIDENTAL

SERIOUSNESS

MILD   MODERATE   SEVERE

FREQUENCY

Very Common 5
Common 4
Uncommon 3
Rare 2
Very Rare 1

PROGNOSIS

GUARDED   POOR   FAIR   GOOD   EXCELLENT

AGE AFFECTED (MONTHS):

0 − 1 − 2 − 3 − 4 − 5 − 6 − 7 − 8 − 9 − 10 − 11 − 12

BREEDS MOST COMMONLY AFFECTED:

Any breed

Clinical Signs

Mild

- Short attacks of sharp inhalations of breath through the nose
- Anxiety
- Pulled back cheeks facial expression

Diagnosis

Most veterinarians will be able to diagnose reverse sneezing through a description of the history or a video of the episode. If accompanied by other signs such as coughing, nasal discharge or a change in voice, your veterinarian may wish to do an examination of the puppy's nose and throat under sedation.

Treatment

No treatment is needed for reverse sneezing.

Prognosis

Reverse sneezing will have no effect on your dog's lifespan or health, and therefore the prognosis is excellent.

Runt of the Litter

About the Condition

The term 'runt of the litter' is not a scientific term, but rather a term to describe one puppy in a litter which is smaller than the rest. The reason for this is unknown, but some people have hypothesized that this is the puppy which was implanted as an embryo in the center of the uterus. Puppies closer to the ovaries are believed to gain more nutrition than the ones in the center; however, this is difficult to prove.

A runt unfortunately has a disadvantage from his littermates. Bigger, stronger puppies are likely to push forward for milk first, meaning that a runt is likely to receive less milk than he needs. As a result, he might fail to thrive. Approximately 17-30% of runts do not survive if action is not taken.

Quick Facts

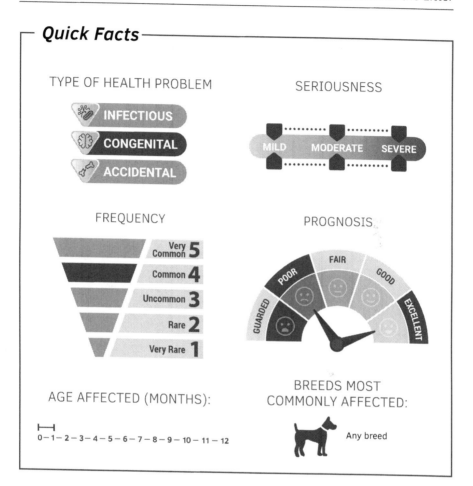

TYPE OF HEALTH PROBLEM

- INFECTIOUS
- CONGENITAL
- ACCIDENTAL

SERIOUSNESS

MILD   MODERATE   SEVERE

FREQUENCY

Very Common	5
Common	4
Uncommon	3
Rare	2
Very Rare	1

PROGNOSIS

GUARDED · POOR · FAIR · GOOD · EXCELLENT

AGE AFFECTED (MONTHS):

0 − 1 − 2 − 3 − 4 − 5 − 6 − 7 − 8 − 9 − 10 − 11 − 12

BREEDS MOST COMMONLY AFFECTED:

Any breed

Clinical Signs

Mild
- Smaller than the other puppies

Moderate
- Last to get milk
- Slow growth

Severe
- Weak
- Rejected by the mother

Diagnosis

When a litter is born, sometimes it is easy to spot the runt, but you should not rely on your observation alone. All puppies should be weighed, and re-weighed 48 hours later to check they are all similar weights, and gaining weight at the same rate.

If there is a particular puppy which is not doing well, the mother and all the puppies should be taken to the vet for a clinical examination.

Treatment

Managing a runt requires intense home care, but if you need additional help, your veterinarian will be able to provide support.

Home Management

Runts which are obviously not growing adequately or having sufficient opportunity to suckle should be removed from the litter and hand-raised by bottle feeding. These puppies are likely to have received an inadequate amount of colostrum from their mother. This is vital for immunity, so it is important to remember that runts will be more susceptible to infectious diseases and parasites.

Prognosis

The prognosis for a runt is either poor or excellent. If spotted too late, the mortality rate is high. However, runts which survive until weaning have an excellent prognosis and, when provided with adequate nutrition, will catch up with the size of their littermates.

Syringomyelia

About the Condition

Syringomyelia is caused by 'caudal occipital malformation syndrome.' This is when there is a malformation in the occipital bone at the back of the skull. As a result, the hole at the back of the skull is crowded, and the cerebellum part of the brain can herniate out of the skull. It is similar to the Chiari type I malformation that occurs in people.

Since there is a crowding in the area due to the malformed skull and cerebellum, cerebrospinal fluid (CSF) flow is disrupted, which leads to the symptoms of the disease. The malformation is present from birth, but symptoms are not usually obvious until adulthood.

Quick Facts

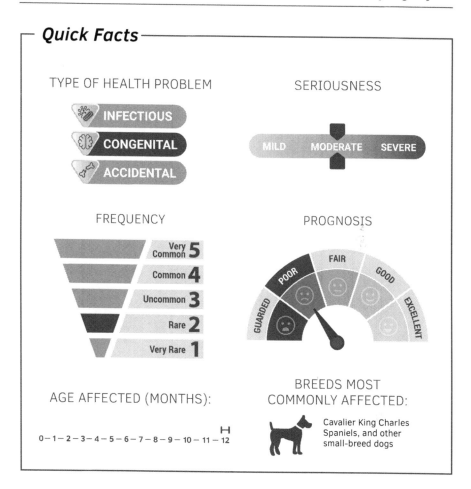

TYPE OF HEALTH PROBLEM

- INFECTIOUS
- CONGENITAL
- ACCIDENTAL

SERIOUSNESS

MILD   MODERATE   SEVERE

FREQUENCY

- Very Common **5**
- Common **4**
- Uncommon **3**
- Rare **2**
- Very Rare **1**

PROGNOSIS

POOR   FAIR   GOOD   GUARDED   EXCELLENT

AGE AFFECTED (MONTHS):

0 – 1 – 2 – 3 – 4 – 5 – 6 – 7 – 8 – 9 – 10 – 11 – 12

BREEDS MOST COMMONLY AFFECTED:

Cavalier King Charles Spaniels, and other small-breed dogs

Clinical Signs

Moderate

- Face rubbing
- Scratching the back of the head
- Loss of balance
- Weakness

Diagnosis

Presumptive diagnosis of syringomyelia can be made based on the breed and symptoms; however, an MRI scan to visualize the brain and skull will give a definitive diagnosis.

Treatment

Treatment can be variable, and should be under the guidance of a veterinary neurology specialist.

Medical Management

Medical management is not usually effective, but can be attempted with gabapentin to reduce the sensations of itchiness on the face and back of the head. Omeprazole can also decrease the production of CSF. Pain relief is also vital.

Surgical Management

Surgery is technical and requires decompression of the area through removing a small part of the skull.

Prognosis

The prognosis is poor as medical management is not often effective, and recurrence rates after surgery are between 25% and 47%.

Teething

About the Condition

All puppies go through the process of teething. This is when their deciduous (baby) teeth fall out and adult teeth grow in their place. For most puppies, this starts at eight weeks and goes on until approximately eight months.

If you're lucky, you won't even know that your puppy is teething. Some puppies show no symptoms and you may never see a fallen-out baby tooth. Other puppies find the discomfort that teething brings difficult to deal with.

Quick Facts

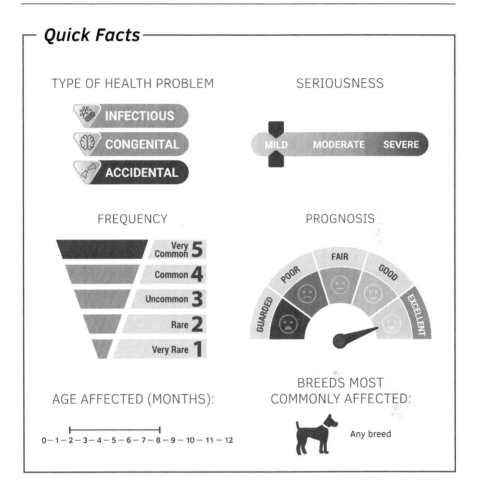

TYPE OF HEALTH PROBLEM

INFECTIOUS

CONGENITAL

ACCIDENTAL

SERIOUSNESS

MILD   MODERATE   SEVERE

FREQUENCY

Very Common **5**
Common **4**
Uncommon **3**
Rare **2**
Very Rare **1**

PROGNOSIS

GUARDED   POOR   FAIR   GOOD   EXCELLENT

AGE AFFECTED (MONTHS):

0 — 1 — 2 — 3 — 4 — 5 — 6 — 7 — 8 — 9 — 10 — 11 — 12

BREEDS MOST COMMONLY AFFECTED:

Any breed

Clinical Signs

Mild

- Red gums
- Chewing on objects
- Drooling
- Spots of blood on chewed items
- Pawing at the mouth

Diagnosis

Diagnosis of teething is easy by looking in your puppy's mouth.

Treatment

Teething doesn't need to be treated by your veterinarian, as there are several things you can do at home to help your puppy's discomfort.

Home Management

Chewing will help soothe the itchiness of your puppy's gums, so left to his own devices, your puppy is likely to chew furniture and other objects around the house. It is best to try to redirect his chewing to appropriate tough chewable toys. Having plenty of options will ensure that he doesn't get bored of one particular toy. Cold toys are also excellent at soothing gums, so putting toys in the fridge for a few hours will help your puppy.

Prognosis

Teething is a process that all puppies must go through. Whether your puppy deals with it well or finds it distressing, once his adult teeth have all come through, he won't have any residual effects.

Traumatic Injuries and Fractures

About the Condition

Puppies love to explore, especially when they have a newfound freedom after their initial vaccinations. But they are still learning what their boundaries and limitations are. As a result, you may find your puppy occasionally gets himself into potentially dangerous situations which can lead to trauma. Road traffic accidents are particularly common in young dogs, so ensuring your dog has a good recall will aid in avoiding a potentially fatal accident.

Trauma can vary from mild bruising, to extensive fractures and blood loss. Internal damage such as diaphragmatic hernias, fractured ribs, burst bladders, bleeding spleens and punctured lungs are all possible without any initial outward signs.

Quick Facts

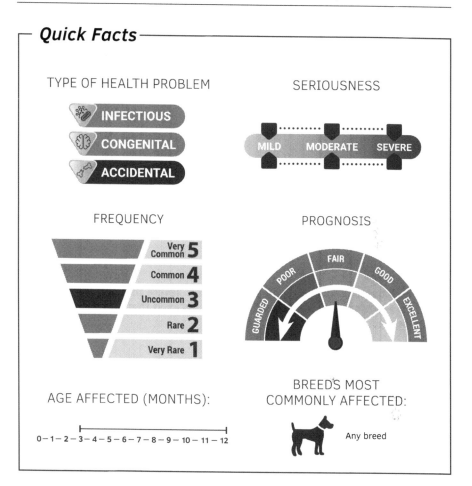

TYPE OF HEALTH PROBLEM

- INFECTIOUS
- CONGENITAL
- ACCIDENTAL

SERIOUSNESS

MILD   MODERATE   SEVERE

FREQUENCY

Very Common **5**
Common **4**
Uncommon **3**
Rare **2**
Very Rare **1**

PROGNOSIS

POOR   FAIR   GOOD
GUARDED   EXCELLENT

AGE AFFECTED (MONTHS):

0 − 1 − 2 − 3 − 4 − 5 − 6 − 7 − 8 − 9 − 10 − 11 − 12

BREED'S MOST COMMONLY AFFECTED:

Any breed

Clinical Signs

Mild

- Bruising
- Scuffed nails
- Minor cuts and abrasions

Moderate

- Lameness
- Muscular injury
- External bleeding
- Bruising
- Bleeding into whites of eyes

221

Umbilical Hernia

About the Condition

Umbilical hernias derive from defects in the abdominal musculature along the midline of the belly. This is where the two sides of the abdominal walls meet, and is called the linea alba. When there is a hole in this area, fat or intestines can push through from inside the abdomen. Umbilical hernias are usually of little concern if they are very small, as only fat can push through. Large hernias are more concerning, as intestines can then come through the hole, but usually then can be pushed back again. It is medium-sized holes which are the most serious, as intestines can come through and become strangled, which is a life-threatening situation.

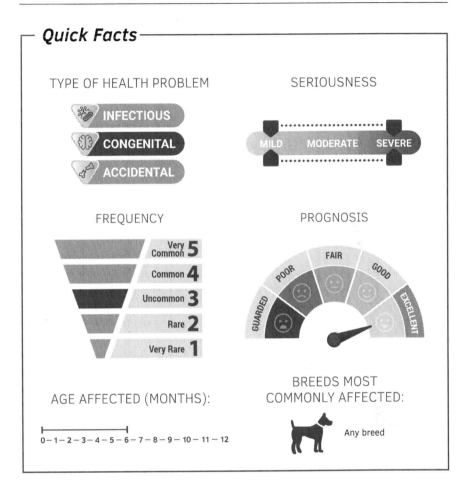

Quick Facts

TYPE OF HEALTH PROBLEM

- INFECTIOUS
- CONGENITAL
- ACCIDENTAL

SERIOUSNESS

MILD   MODERATE   SEVERE

FREQUENCY

- Very Common **5**
- Common **4**
- Uncommon **3**
- Rare **2**
- Very Rare **1**

PROGNOSIS

GUARDED   POOR   FAIR   GOOD   EXCELLENT

AGE AFFECTED (MONTHS):

0 – 1 – 2 – 3 – 4 – 5 – 6 – 7 – 8 – 9 – 10 – 11 – 12

BREEDS MOST COMMONLY AFFECTED:

Any breed

Clinical Signs

Mild

- Non painful, soft bump on the midline of the belly

Severe

- Swollen, hot, or moving bump on the midline of the belly

Diagnosis

Your veterinarian can diagnose an umbilical hernia by looking at and feeling the bump. He may perform an ultrasound scan to determine if intestines or fat are involved.

Treatment

Surgical Management

Hernias are usually surgically repaired at the same time as neutering, around six to nine months of age, unless they are potentially strangling the intestines.

Prognosis

Once surgically repaired, there will be no lasting consequences from the hernia. However, dogs which have had hernias should not be bred as the condition is thought to be congenital.

Undescended Testicles

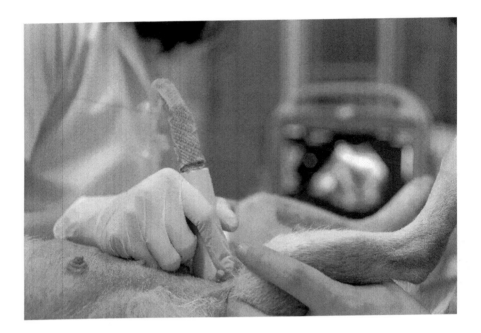

About the Condition

When one or both testicles have not descended, it is known as cryptorchidism. It is the most common genital development problem of dogs. Genetics play a major role; however, it is hypothesized that there are some environmental factors involved too. If both testicles are undescended, it is likely to result in sterility.

The undescended testicle will be located anywhere between the kidney and the scrotum, and is commonly found in the inguinal canal, a narrow opening between the abdomen and the scrotum. These testicles can still produce hormones.

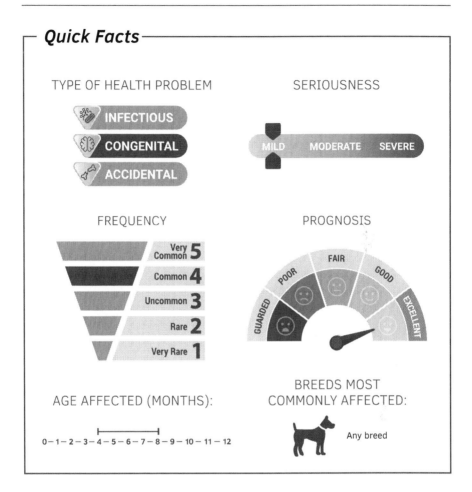

Quick Facts

TYPE OF HEALTH PROBLEM

- INFECTIOUS
- CONGENITAL
- ACCIDENTAL

SERIOUSNESS

MILD — MODERATE — SEVERE

FREQUENCY

- Very Common 5
- Common 4
- Uncommon 3
- Rare 2
- Very Rare 1

PROGNOSIS

GUARDED — POOR — FAIR — GOOD — EXCELLENT

AGE AFFECTED (MONTHS):

0 − 1 − 2 − 3 − 4 − 5 − 6 − 7 − 8 − 9 − 10 − 11 − 12

BREEDS MOST COMMONLY AFFECTED:

Any breed

Clinical Signs

Mild

• Lack of two testicles in the scrotum by four months old

Diagnosis

Your veterinarian will feel your dog's scrotum for the presence of two testicles. If only one or none is present, he is likely to perform an ultrasound scan to determine where the testicle is located.

Treatment

Surgical Management

Undescended testicles should always be surgically removed as they are at higher risk to develop testicular cancers such as seminomas and interstitial cell tumors.

Prognosis

Once the testicle is removed, your dog will not have any ill health effects; however, since there is a genetic link, he should never be bred if the normal testicle was not also removed at the same time.

Urinary Tract Infections

About the Condition

Urinary tract infections are usually caused by bacteria which have ascended up the urethra to the bladder. Both males and females can be affected. In female puppies, juvenile vaginitis and urinary tract infections can appear very similar.

Quick Facts

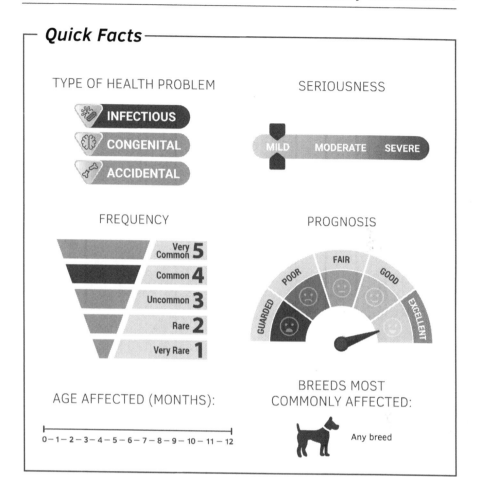

TYPE OF HEALTH PROBLEM

- INFECTIOUS
- CONGENITAL
- ACCIDENTAL

SERIOUSNESS

MILD | MODERATE | SEVERE

FREQUENCY

- Very Common **5**
- Common **4**
- Uncommon **3**
- Rare **2**
- Very Rare **1**

PROGNOSIS

GUARDED | POOR | FAIR | GOOD | EXCELLENT

AGE AFFECTED (MONTHS):

0 — 1 — 2 — 3 — 4 — 5 — 6 — 7 — 8 — 9 — 10 — 11 — 12

BREEDS MOST COMMONLY AFFECTED:

Any breed

Clinical Signs

Mild

- Frequent urination
- Passing only small amounts of urine
- Smelly urine
- Urine with blood in it
- Licking genitals
- Urinating in the house even though housebroken
- Leaking urine

Diagnosis

A urinary tract infection can be diagnosed with a sample of urine. Your vet will analyze it with several tests. Firstly, a dipstick test will check for white blood cells, protein and blood which indicate inflammation, and pH which becomes higher and

233

more alkaline when there is an infection. Next, a specific gravity test will check how concentrated the urine is, which indicates whether the kidneys are working to full capacity. And finally, microscopy will check for crystals which can cause additional damage and inflammation.

If this is all normal, your vet may decide to insert contrast into the bladder to be able to see it clearly on an X-ray, or he may do an ultrasound on the bladder.

Treatment

Urinary tract infections usually clear up quickly with appropriate treatment, so if the treatment doesn't seem to be working, you should revisit your vet to make sure the diagnosis is correct. Other disorders such as urinary stones, juvenile vaginitis, and ectopic ureters, can look similar to urinary tract infections so it is easy for a misdiagnosis to be made.

Home Management

Encouraging your dog to drink plenty of water will dilute his urine. This will provide comfort for him as urine can cause the inflamed lining of the bladder to become even more sore.

Medical Management

Your veterinarian will prescribe antibiotics and anti-inflammatories if he has diagnosed a urinary tract infection.

Prognosis

The prognosis after a urinary tract infection is excellent as it rarely has any lasting effects.

Ventricular Septal Defect

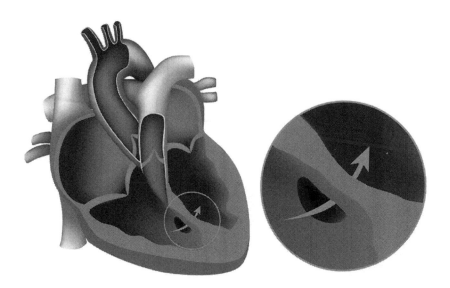

About the Condition

The heart is split into two halves; the left and the right. Each half is then further split into the atria at the top and the ventricles at the bottom. In between the two halves is a muscular division called the septum. A ventricular septal defect occurs when there is a hole in the septum at the level of the ventricles, allowing the blood to shunt from one side of the heart to the other, through the hole.

Blood usually shunts from the left side of the heart to the right side, as the muscles of the left side are larger, and therefore the pressure from the heart beat is greater. This can lead to severe circulatory derangements and dilation of the heart due to an excessive pressure load.

Unlike other types of heart conditions, the louder the accompanying heart murmur, the smaller the hole and therefore the smaller the problem.

Quick Facts

TYPE OF HEALTH PROBLEM

SERIOUSNESS

FREQUENCY

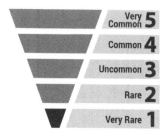

PROGNOSIS

AGE AFFECTED (MONTHS):

0 − 1 − 2 − 3 − 4 − 5 − 6 − 7 − 8 − 9 − 10 − 11 − 12

BREEDS MOST COMMONLY AFFECTED:

Any breed, especially English Springer Spaniels

Clinical Signs

Mild

- No symptoms
- Loud murmur

Moderate

- Fast heart rate

Severe

- Exercise intolerance
- Fast breathing
- Coughing
- Blue gums (cyanosis)
- Quiet murmur

Diagnosis

The best method to diagnose a ventricular septal defect is with echocardiography, otherwise known as a heart ultrasound. This will allow the veterinarian to visualize and measure the hole in the septum.

Treatment

Treatment depends on the severity of the symptoms and the direction in which the blood is shunting. If the defect is very small, no treatment is necessary.

Medical Management

For moderate and severe ventricular septal defects, heart medication to improve the pumping and reduce pressure on the heart and lungs is needed to prevent heart failure.

Surgical Management

If the defect is large, and the blood shunts from the left to the right, the defect can be surgically closed. Heart surgery has to be performed by a specialist, as it requires extensive training and equipment.

Prognosis

Small defects have an excellent prognosis, even without treatment. However large defects, unless surgically closed, and defects where the blood goes from the right to the left side of the heart, carry a guarded or poor prognosis for the future.

Worms

About the Condition

There are two types of worms your puppy might pick up early in their life, which have been discussed further in Section 2; roundworms and tapeworms. While your puppy can pick up worms any time in his life, he is most susceptible in the first six months, and especially the first three.

Roundworms are more common for puppies to become infected with than tape-worms, and both can be detrimental. Worms live in the intestines and not only cause damage to the intestinal wall linings, but also steal the nutrients from the food which has been ingested, which can lead to malnutrition in addition to other symptoms.

Quick Facts

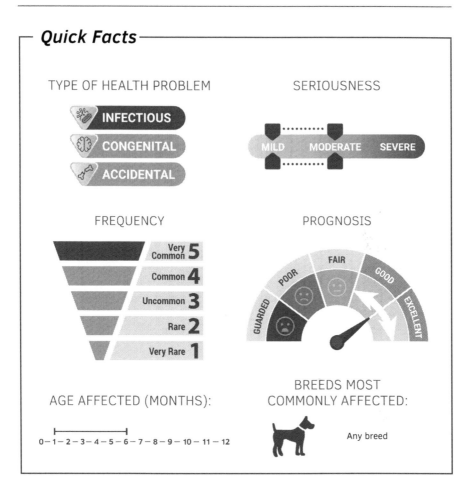

TYPE OF HEALTH PROBLEM

- INFECTIOUS
- CONGENITAL
- ACCIDENTAL

SERIOUSNESS

MILD · MODERATE · SEVERE

FREQUENCY

- Very Common **5**
- Common **4**
- Uncommon **3**
- Rare **2**
- Very Rare **1**

PROGNOSIS

GUARDED · POOR · FAIR · GOOD · EXCELLENT

AGE AFFECTED (MONTHS):

0 — 1 — 2 — 3 — 4 — 5 — 6 — 7 — 8 — 9 — 10 — 11 — 12

BREEDS MOST COMMONLY AFFECTED:

Any breed

Clinical Signs

Mild

- None
- Diarrhea

Moderate

- Vomiting
- Potbelly
- Malnutrition
- Weakness
- Dehydration
- Dull coat

Diagnosis

Sometimes worms can be seen in the feces, but often a fecal sample needs to be taken in order to diagnosis the condition for certain. This is done by means of a flotation test, where the fecal material is mixed with a solution and then filtered. It is then left to stand to allow worm eggs to float to the top. These can then be analyzed under the microscope.

Treatment

It is possible to buy worming treatment over the counter, as it is not always licensed as a prescription product, but if your puppy is experiencing symptoms, he should have prescribed medication.

Medical Management

De-worming treatments can come in the form of a paste, tablet or spot-on pipette. They should be given to puppies every two weeks until 12 weeks of age, and monthly thereafter. Once your puppy is over six months, he can be treated every three months for worms, unless you live in a heartworm endemic area, and then he must have more frequent treatments.

Prognosis

Most worm infections easily clear up with treatment with no long-lasting effects, but for more serious infections, there may be long-lasting damage to the intestine walls, which can lead to life-long gut sensitivity.

Made in the USA
Coppell, TX
18 January 2023

11329119R00133